WHAT GOD
HAS BROUGHT
ME THROUGH

WHAT GOD HAS BROUGHT ME THROUGH

MY INSPIRATION TO OTHERS

THOMAS DYKES SR.

WHAT GOD HAS BROUGHT ME THROUGH MY INSPIRATION TO OTHERS

iUniverse books may be ordered through booksellers or by contacting:

iUniverse
1663 Liberty Drive
Bloomington, IN 47403
www.iuniverse.com
1-800-Authors (1-800-288-4677)

Because of the dynamic nature of the Internet, any web addresses or links contained in this book may have changed since publication and may no longer be valid. The views expressed in this work are solely those of the author and do not necessarily reflect the views of the publisher, and the publisher hereby disclaims any responsibility for them.

Any people depicted in stock imagery provided by Thinkstock are models, and such images are being used for illustrative purposes only. Certain stock imagery © Thinkstock.

Scripture quotations marked KJV are from the Holy Bible, King James Version (Authorized Version). First published in 1611. Quoted from the KJV Classic Reference Bible, Copyright © 1983 by The Zondervan Corporation.

Scripture quotations marked NKJV are taken from the New King James Version. Copyright © 1982 by Thomas Nelson, Inc. Used by permission. All rights reserved.

ISBN: 978-1-5320-3846-4 (sc)
ISBN: 978-1-5320-3844-0 (hc)
ISBN: 978-1-5320-3845-7 (e)

Library of Congress Control Number: 2017918770

Print information available on the last page.

iUniverse rev. date: 12/18/2017

I can do all things through Christ which strengthens me.

—Philippians 4:13

PREFACE

I am an African American who was born into a large family and who grew up in Philadelphia's inner city. In this book I will recount what I accomplished in my youth, in the navy, in the aeronautical industry, in the construction field, and beyond. In each job I have held, God has blessed me with the ability to perform in a professional way and has allowed me to gain recognition for my achievements. This is the story of what God has brought me through in my life.

CHAPTER 1

I was born in South Philadelphia on August 2, 1951, and grew up in the inner city in an African American family. I have four brothers and three sisters, including my twin. We were raised in a two-parent home. Our father worked hard as a laborer for the Philadelphia Gas Company. Our mother was a homemaker/housewife who stayed at home to care for us children.

When I was five or six years old, we were living on Lawrence Street in South Philly, not far from my paternal grandfather. He was very old, lived alone, and cared for himself, even doing his own cooking. He played the fiddle and was trying to teach my oldest sister how to play it. Before he passed away, he gave her the instrument.

One day when we were quite young, my twin sister and I were playing in the backyard of our Lawrence Street home. When our mother called us in to have lunch, my sister said to me, "I'll race you into the house. Let's see who can get there first." As I was running, I slipped and fell on the steps and split my head open. I felt like all the blood was leaving my body as it poured from my head. I thought I was going to die. My mother dressed the cut and took me to the hospital. The emergency room staff cleaned out the cut, gave me stitches, bandaged me up, and sent us home. The injury could have been worse, and I thank God for watching over me.

We soon moved to another area of South Philly, renting a three-story house on Kenilworth Street with plenty of room for all of us. We experienced strange events in that house and suspected that it was haunted. In the front living room, we would hear snoring and heavy breathing when no one was there. Then one of my sisters was given an old doll by a neighbor who was in her seventies or eighties. Several times my sister put the doll on the first floor by the stairs only to wake up in the morning or sometimes at night to find the doll at the foot of her bed or beside the bed, facing her. None of us ever moved the doll, as she thought. With all the odd things happening in the house, we moved after only a few months.

We relocated across town to Gaskill Street between Lombard and South Streets and between Third and Fourth Streets. It took several trips to bring everything to our new home. My siblings and I were happy in this diverse neighborhood. Our parents always made sure we lived in mixed-race neighborhoods with people of many nationalities. They believed we should learn how to relate to those of other racial and ethnic backgrounds. This taught us a better way of life and brought us greater success throughout our lives. All the residents of Gaskill Street respected one another.

In the late fifties and early sixties, a state program called Surplus helped feed large families. Families would get vouchers for surplus food, with the amounts based on family size. Many families received this assistance, which was badly needed and greatly appreciated. Families could pick up surplus food at a designated time and place each month. The program made it somewhat easier for low-income providers to feed their families.

While we were living on Gaskill Street, all of us children were assigned chores and were expected to do them every day. Our parents instilled in us the importance of personal responsibility and of performing these tasks with pride and with respect for others. We were in church every Sunday and participated in many church functions. My brothers and I joined the Boys Club, and my sisters joined the Pioneer Girls Club. At age twelve, I accepted the Lord as my personal savior and asked him to come into my heart. I was baptized after completing the requirements. We all attended church regularly; we were grateful to learn about God's Word and enjoyed the fellowship.

I attended McCall Elementary School, located at Sixth and Delaney Streets in South Philly. When I was in the fourth or fifth grade, I joined the safety patrol and became a crossing guard. I would direct other children across the street, watching the traffic to make sure everyone would be safe. The job gave me the desire to inspire people when I grew up. I served in the safety patrol until about 1960 or '61, when I learned auditions would be held for the All-Philadelphia Boys Choir that would soon be formed. I decided to try out for the choir.

I was intrigued by the possibility of using my God-given talent to sing. I auditioned and was accepted as an alto. Our conductor was Dr. Carlton Lake. My older sister made sure I attended the rehearsals on Saturday mornings at Ben Franklin High School in North Philly. She drove me to every rehearsal rain or shine. During the early sixties when I was a member, the choir toured, sang at places throughout the city, and recorded an album.

I sang with the All-Philadelphia Boys Choir until I became a teen and my voice changed. I was then asked to join the All-Philadelphia Junior Choir, but I declined the offer to start an after-school job. At this point, I was in the sixth grade. Our music teacher had something special he wanted our graduating class to perform. He was Italian and loved Italian opera. His plan was to teach the class several Italian opera selections for the sixth-grade commencement exercises. We knew this would be a challenge, mainly because we didn't speak or understand the language. The pieces we were to sing were composed by Giuseppe Verdi. Our teacher taught us the correct pronunciation of the Italian and discussed the plots of the operas. To his amazement and ours, we sang the selections flawlessly. Our parents and others who attended the graduation exercises were pleasantly surprised by our performance. Having completed sixth grade, I headed for junior high school.

CHAPTER 2

I attended Furness Junior High School, located at Third and Mifflin Streets. The actor and comedian Joey Bishop had graduated from Furness many years earlier. My twin sister and I were excited about attending the school and would often walk there from our home on Gaskill Street. It was a long hike across town, but we didn't mind.

Our friends would walk to school with us, so we thought walking was a lot of fun and preferred it to taking the bus. We had a great time growing up in the house on Gaskill Street and made a lot of friends with children who lived on nearby streets. An African American couple had several children around the same age as my twin sister and me. Other friends lived around the corner on South Street and on Lombard Street.

My twin sister and I, along with friends from Gaskill Street, would go roller-skating. We had the old metal skates with the metal key that we would use to tighten and lock the skates. We would skate every day, so our skates would run down pretty quickly. But we never wasted anything. When our skates ran down to the point where we couldn't get a good roll out of them, we would break down the skates, split them in half, and make a skateboard with a wooden crate—half of the skate in the front and half in the back. We would nail down the crate, placing a stick up front to help us steer. This was a lot of fun.

As kids we did a lot of exploring. We used to take trips up South Street, or we would go a little farther to Chestnut Street or Market Street. We would test out our skates and see how far or how fast we could go. Sometimes we would even journey to Washington Avenue, a busy area, especially in those days. We would skate down South Street Hill, or we would skate all the way down to Front Street from

Washington Avenue, just about to the river. The ships would come in and would off-load supplies, sometimes leaving them out on the docks.

My twin sister and I called ourselves explorers because we would explore the city. We would walk from our house to the Academy of Natural Sciences and then to the Franklin Institute. We would stop along the way to visit the Betsy Ross House, Alfred's Alley, and other historical sites and museums. We would visit the parks, play on the monuments down in Center City, and see the Liberty Bell, which was in a different location than it is now. The Atwater Kent museum was our favorite museum downtown. There was no cost to visit any of the museums. We would view the historical exhibits, and these things would stay fixed in our memories. My sister and I did this every weekend, winter and summer, and we were never bored. We always had something to do.

We used to visit friends who lived on South Street between Fourth and Third Streets. They had a pretty large basement, and when the weather was bad and we couldn't skate outdoors, we would skate there. It was like skating at a rink. We continued to explore from South Philly to North Philly, and we enjoyed it. When the Hopkins House was being constructed in the Society Hill area of South Philly, the builders made a big dirt hill. My sister and I would climb this hill, and in the winter when it snowed, we would slide down the hill on our sleds. We would always be outside whenever it snowed. I'll never forget one really bad winter in the 1960s. There was such a large accumulation of snow that my twin sister and I made a snow cave next to our house. It took a couple of days to construct, and when we had finished, we hung out inside where it was warm. One day we started to tear it down because the temperature was rising and the snow cave was melting. My sister lost her boot, and we never found it even after the snow vanished. Somehow that boot disappeared. It was a mystery how something could just disappear like that, but at least we had fun. We played with our neighbors, we had plenty of friends and plenty of things to do, and there was never a dull moment.

I joined the Boy Scouts with my best friend and found the activities very interesting. We would attend meetings every Friday evening at Father Divine Church on South Broad Street. We were taught the Scout oath and learned about the merit badges we could earn. These could be put on our sashes. We also attended jamborees and summer camps where we would do knot tying, enjoy canoeing and rowboating, and learn about nature. Besides becoming an Eagle Scout, every Boy Scout wanted to gain membership in the Order of the Arrow, and achieving that recognition involved many steps. After one of our Friday Boy Scout meetings, my best friend asked me if I'd like to drive with him, his parents, his sister, and his brother to the Audubon Shopping Center in New Jersey. They did this every Friday after our meeting. I asked my parents, and they gave me permission, so I was able to do that.

As we grew older, my friend and I went our separate ways. By this time, I was collecting newspapers, taking them to a junkyard, and getting paid based on the weight of the paper. I also used to collect cardboard, rags, and any other junk I could sell. The times were pretty hard, but I stayed busy. I always wanted to have my own money. After we reached a certain age, all of us children decided to get jobs so we could have a little extra money for ourselves. We gave our mom some of what we earned. It was good to work and to make our own money and to do what we wanted with it. Self-reliance was instilled in us as kids.

As a young boy, I would look for spare wood in stores and bring it home to help fire up our stove. We had a coal furnace and radiators in the rooms. Steam would accumulate in the radiators, creating heat throughout the house. Whenever the fire in the furnace was out, we'd have to start it. We couldn't fire up the coal without first having a bed of fire started with wood. It was my job to make sure we kept wood in the house, and I would check to see if there was enough in the basement to restart a fire. We would have coal delivered to the house whenever we ran out, maybe once a month. We would open a basement window in the front of the house, and the deliveryman would send the coal through a chute into a bin. We would then shovel the coal from the bin into the furnace. Each of us boys had to learn how to do this.

As a young boy, I didn't know I would get the chance to operate the coal furnace, but I learned to do this when I got bit older. I was then responsible for maintaining and operating the furnace. In time I learned to enjoy that responsibility. My twin sister and I continued to explore the city, and we joined the Barns Center on Pine Street. The center was a Catholic-run recreational facility where kids in the area could meet. We enjoyed the Barns Center but eventually stopped going. We kept touring historical places. We visited Mother Bethel AME Church quite often. We were interested in learning about Richard Allen. Born in February 1760, he was an African American bishop and a founder of the African Methodist Episcopal Church. He was also a writer and an educator. He qualified as a preacher in 1784. Richard Allen is entombed in a basement at Mother Bethel AME Church. As always, we were explorers for information and wanted to learn and to understand history.

CHAPTER 3

I landed my first job in a clothing store on Fourth and South Streets. I got this job because my brother used to work there and moved on to another job. I worked at the clothing store for two summers and was able to put away money. I had always hoped to have my own money to buy things I wanted and needed, so I worked for it. Looking for a job that would pay me more money, I got work at a drugstore. I thought helping people out would be a great way to learn customer service. Because of the way I presented myself to him and to the customers, the store owner began to show great faith in me. I was the first African American male to have worked in the drugstore. I got to know almost all of the regular customers by name. Most were elderly, and they appreciated the help I gave them finding the many items in the store.

The owner eventually trusted me to run the store while he was out. He took me to the places where we ordered many of our supplies and introduced me to the vendors. He trusted me enough to send me to South Street to pick up items for the store. One day I was returning empty-handed because the supply house didn't have what we needed. As I headed down South Seventh Street, I saw five to eight young black males walking down the street. I heard one of them say, "There's one. Let's get him." I realized they were a gang and looking for trouble. I knew the city had gangs that would fight one another. I never belonged to a gang. I took off when these guys started chasing me. I believed that I was running for my life and that I would be killed if I stopped. As one of my pursuers got closer, I felt something stick me in the back and then in the ear. I continued to run, as it seemed the gang was catching up to me. I felt like I had been stabbed with a large knife, and I thought my ear was gone, but I didn't stop running.

I didn't feel any blood coming from my body or any faintness due to loss of blood. I knew these guys were after me, but I didn't know what they wanted. I assumed they were trying to kill me. Finally, I noticed no one was chasing me any longer, so I slowed down. At this point, I was about a block away from the drugstore. As I walked toward the drugstore, a woman who usually came to the store each day saw me as she stood on the steps and screamed, "Oh my God, you are full of blood." I didn't know I was bleeding; I just felt tired from running. As I entered the store, my boss saw the blood running down my back and down the right side of my face. He immediately called the police. The police came, and an ambulance arrived to take me to the hospital. The police asked me if I was part of a gang, and I said I wasn't. My boss vouched for me. The police thought it was odd that I had been attacked, but I said these guys may have assumed I was part of another gang in that area of the city. I had been stabbed three times in the back and once in the ear with an ice pick. At the hospital, I got stitched up and received some shots and was on my way.

My mother had told me several times before, "Watch how you dress and how you carry yourself, because people are often mistaken for others based on the way they look or on how they dress." She had a point because the guys who were chasing me were all were dressed in a similar way. I knew gang members sometimes dressed alike. They would wear certain types of jackets or hats or other garments to show they were part of a gang. I was wearing my regular clothes. I wore nothing that would associate me with a gang. I believe the guys who attacked me were just out to hurt somebody and didn't care who that person might be. I continued to work at the drugstore despite the attack. I thanked God for protecting me and keeping me from further harm. When I was ready to leave my job at the drugstore, I gave my boss plenty of notice, and I referred a friend of mine for the job once I had left.

I got a job at the Italian market on Ninth Street, working in a restaurant that sold steak, roast pork, and roast beef sandwiches, and hoagies. The place also had a soda fountain. I was just beginning high school, and I took the job to make extra money on the weekends.

The owner and I got along well. He hired me because of my friendly disposition, and he felt I would probably be good at serving people. I worked at the restaurant for quite a while, mainly on Friday nights after school. Everybody shopped at the Italian market on Saturday. I would go in Friday night and help the owner prepare for a very busy day.

CHAPTER 4

In September 1965 I started class at Bok Vocational Technical High School at Eighth and Mifflin Streets. I had training in carpentry while attending Furness Junior High School. At Bok I studied English, math, history, and science in the morning, and in the early afternoon I took a carpentry and cabinetmaking class. My instructor was a carpenter and a cabinetmaker, so he found it easy to teach the course. He used his knowledge along with the curriculum the school had set up, and he did this well. We started off with basic instruction, learning about the many joints used in the carpentry trade, particularly in cabinetmaking. If you look at a piece of furniture, especially a well-constructed one, you'll see a lot of those joints.

Before we made these joints, we learned about the hand tools used in the carpentry and cabinetmaking trade. Once we knew about these tools, we were instructed on how to make the joints. We were each given a block of wood to make a joint. When the joint was finished, we would take it to the instructor and have him inspect it. If the joint was made correctly, we were given another block of wood to make another joint. If the joint wasn't satisfactory, the instructor would throw it away and tell us to do it again. Some of my classmates didn't feel comfortable with the instructor throwing away something they had tried hard to make, but he was teaching us that we had to learn to do things professionally. He tried to instill in us that we had to do a job perfectly, and he taught us things about the trade that we would not forget. As journeymen in the carpentry and cabinetmaking trade, and in other trades we might pick up, we would always remember the professionalism we were taught.

Once we had completed making all of the joints required in

carpentry and cabinetmaking, we learned about power machinery used in the trade. Many of these electric tools were at our disposal in the shop. We were taught how to use all hand and power tools, and there were many. We were also taught how to improvise with what we had, something a tradesman must learn to do. A tradesman may not always have the correct tool for the job, but if he knows the trade he can do the job with what he's got. I've experienced that situation. We were also taught how to read a blueprint. We went on to construct a one-level house. The school's wood shop was big enough to accommodate that house. We started with the floor installation, followed by the walls, the windows, the doors, and the ceiling. I thought this was a very interesting and helpful project. This was something we could use when we got out of school and entered the building trade or went into cabinetmaking or other trades.

I picked things up pretty quickly. I excelled in the carpentry and cabinetmaking class, and my teacher appointed me as shop foreman. My job was to help the other students with any issues such as blueprint reading and questions about materials. I worked alongside my teacher, helping to instruct the rest of the class. After school hours I bought tools of my own. I wanted to do remodeling or whatever else I could do to make extra money. My teacher had told me there was good money to be made. He said I should always be sure to do a good job because that way people would use me again and would refer other people to me. I kept that in my heart. Before you know it, I ran into a lady I knew in South Philly. She wanted to know if I could install floor tile in her house, and I told her, "Sure, I can do it." I said I would contact her when I was ready to measure the floor and would explain how I would price the job. I was very excited about this opportunity, so when I got to school I talked to my shop teacher about the job. He gave me all the information I needed to start the job and told me how to charge the lady and how to do the work.

I saw the lady the next day and told her what I would charge for the work and how long it would take, and she said she wanted me to do the job. That was my first job as a carpenter. I thanked God for giving me the wisdom and the knowledge to reason and to figure things out. I laid out the room the woman wanted done and put down the tile. My first job was flawless. The lady was happy with my work and offered me another job. I was very excited about that because this was my first job and I'd never laid floor tile before. I told my shop teacher the news, and he was pleased to hear that I had done well on this first job and that I had been offered another job.

I picked out the materials I would need for the next job. The lady wanted me to take down an old set of stairs and to install a new set. One weekend I had helped my teacher do the same job at someone else's house, so I knew exactly how to get started and how to go about doing this. One of my classmates was also a skilled carpenter, and I hired him to help me. We finished on a Saturday, and the woman was again pleased. She said she would refer me to friends who might need work done in their houses, and I thanked her for that.

I learned something new in class every week, and I got better at carpentry and cabinetmaking. I made several pieces of furniture for my mom and for my older sister. I also made a set of chess pieces for some nuns, using a wood lathe in the shop. The job was very tricky and very hard, and I wasted a lot of wood, but it was an interesting experience. My skills in the trade improved as time went by.

My shop teacher took me and another guy from our class on jobs with him. He had jobs to do at businesses and at homes. I'll never forget a job we did for a loan company on North Broad Street in Philly. We installed a new terrazzo floor, and I never knew what terrazzo was until we started that job. It looked beautiful. We did a lot of cabinet work, countertops, and other carpentry. I worked with my teacher almost every weekend and learned a lot about the trade from him. We never had to return to fix any job we did. Each job had to be done right the first time. I learned that if you do a job right, you're contented and the customer is contented, and you never have to worry about going back and fixing something you should have done right the first time. That lesson stayed with me throughout my life. I continue to give God glory and praise for instilling these things in me and for giving me the wisdom and the understanding to make things work and to do a good job the first time.

I worked with my shop teacher on Friday nights and Saturdays, never working on Sundays because the Lord's Day was dedicated to church. It was a blessing for me to learn as much as I did in that four-year period. I learned there was more to the carpentry trade than just carpentry. We were taught in carpentry class that there were other trades involved in construction. Electrical, plumbing, HVAC, and masonry all go into building. We were given some understanding of those other trades. When we got out into the world, we remembered something about those trades and could use that knowledge.

Attending Bok was an awesome experience. I'm sure everyone who went there remembers Red's Hoagie Shop across the street from the school. Everyone loved Red's hoagies. We used to sneak out from the back of the school and go over to grab them. This way we would have them ahead of time. We knew Red's would be crowded at lunchtime and we probably wouldn't be able to get there, buy a hoagie, and return to school before the period was over. That's why many students at Bok would sneak out or would send someone else to get hoagies.

I was now in my third year of carpentry and cabinetmaking class. I was doing very well and my grades were excellent. My carpentry teacher asked me and three classmates if we would be interested in full-time jobs. A school program would allow us to go to work in the twelfth grade. We would not have to come to school, but our work performance would be noted on our report cards. The four of us accepted the offer and were hired to work for a company in Glenside, Pennsylvania, that made wooden missile crates for the navy and wooden pallets for companies that shipped products all over the country.

We were all very excited about working forty hours a week and getting paychecks. We were trained and assigned positions at the company. However, the other three guys were lax, spending a lot of time in the bathroom and taking plenty of breaks. The shop foreman would walk through the plant, checking everyone's progress, and he would see that I was constantly working. I took few breaks and did what I was asked to do. One day the foreman asked if I would like to run a saw at the end of the shop. The position he was offering me involved measuring and cutting lumber at specific lengths. One of the guys doing this work was ready to retire, and the shop foreman was looking for someone to replace him.

I was amazed that the foreman had offered me the job. He said he had been watching me and my work habits, as well as my performance. I told him I would be more than happy to take the job, and I thanked him. He also mentioned I would get a pay increase, and I was very grateful for that. When I started the job, directly across from me was a much older worker who had been with the company for many years. He instructed me on work procedures and showed me how to operate the saw, and I was grateful for those instructions. I did my share of work and more. One day to my surprise, the foreman told me he was giving me a fifty-cent raise. He said I deserved it because I was doing a very good job. I thanked him, and I thanked God. I showed up for work on time every day, didn't take many breaks, and put out what I had to put out in a short time. I performed so well that one day the foreman said, "You can take two days off with pay because you've cut enough material to keep the men busy for a couple of days." I was thankful to be given time off with pay.

The veteran worker across from me commended me and told me to keep up the good work. A few months later, the foreman gave me another raise and commended me once again. He told me the company would be laying off workers but said I didn't have to worry about that. A day or two later, my three classmates got pink slips. They asked me if I had gotten one, and I said no. They were surprised and disappointed to have been let go. No matter where you are, no matter where you work, if you do your job professionally, you won't have a problem keeping that job. That was my experience.

When my classmates got laid off, I was the only high school kid working in the plant. All the other workers were grown men, but I didn't feel bad about that. I saw myself as one of the guys. I did my job every day, and the foreman was pleased with my work. When the holidays came, the company gave out bonuses to the workers, and I received what the other men received. The company also gave each man a turkey. Even though I was a teenager in high school, I was appreciated as much as the other workers, and I was thankful for that. One day the owner of the company called me into his office and said I had been doing an excellent job. He had gotten a good report about me from the foreman, and he told me to keep up the good work. That conversation stuck with me and I felt good about it.

My high school days were nearing an end, and I was getting ready for the senior prom. I was also thinking about a few things I would like to do in the future. I had always wanted to fly, and I thought about joining the navy. I didn't talk to anybody about this. One day I stopped by at the navy recruitment office on South Broad Street and spoke to one of the recruiters. I told him I would love to fly, and he gave me a bunch of information about what I could do in the navy. He emphasized that I had to do well on the navy entrance exam because my score would help determine my classification in the navy. A good score could help me enter whatever field I desired once I joined the military. I wanted to fly, so I kept that advice in mind.

My senior prom was a beautiful event; it was held on an old ship docked by what we now call Penn's Landing in South Philly. After the prom we all had our own ideas about where we were going. My date and I and my twin sister and her date ended up going to the Hawaiian Cottage on Route 38 in Cherry Hill, New Jersey. From there, we went to the Latin Casino. We enjoyed ourselves. Many other class members headed to the Boardwalk in Atlantic City. Most of the students were from Philly, and many had never visited Atlantic City. That night they wanted to go there to see what it was like.

CHAPTER 5

When I graduated from high school in June 1969, the country was at war in Vietnam. The tragedies of the war were on everyone's mind, but I still wanted to join the navy because I had a thirst for flying. After graduation, I continued to work for the company in Glenside, Pennsylvania, before I enlisted in the navy. When I told my parents that I wanted to go into the service, they weren't happy about it because they knew this was wartime. My older brother, who attended the prom with me, had already enlisted in the army. He had gone to boot camp and had been sent to Vietnam, so my parents were even more worried when I said I wanted to join the navy. I explained to them that this was what I wanted to do. I wanted to fly, and I told them I had a better chance of doing that if I enlisted instead of waiting for a draft notice. There wasn't too much they could say. I had made my decision.

I was on a 180-day-delay program, meaning it would be 180 days before I would enter the navy. I believe the delay was part of navy recruiting procedures. I continued to work in Glenside, but I told the owner of the company that I had enlisted in the navy and that I would be leaving for boot camp in February 1970. He was happy to hear that I wanted to serve my country, and he said that because I was a good worker, my job would still be available once I left the service. I greatly appreciated his kind words and his generous offer. When the time neared for me to go to boot camp, I gave the company my resignation, and everyone wished me well. A few days after leaving my job, I had to pack and prepare myself for the journey to boot camp. My mother baked cookies for me. She and my twin sister took me to the Thirtieth

Street station where I was to board a train on the first leg of my journey to Great Lakes, Michigan, for boot camp.

This was a very trying time for me. I didn't know what lay ahead at boot camp, and I had never been away from my mom and the rest of my family. I boarded the train and got seated, and as the train pulled away from the station, my mother and my sister waved goodbye. I noticed the tears in their eyes as they waved to me. I felt like I would never see them again, and perhaps they felt the same. My mother was a praying mother, and I know she prayed to God to protect me and to bring me back home safe. My mother prayed continually for all of her children.

As I sat on the train, I thought about my ex-girlfriend. She and I belonged to a church on Fourth and Bainbridge Streets in South Philly. When I told her I was going into the navy, she told me she didn't want to be my girlfriend anymore because she was afraid something might happen to me. She said I might get killed in the war, and she didn't think she could live with that. So she decided to break it off between us. This happened just before I left for boot camp. I was heading to boot camp, and I didn't have a girlfriend to write. I would have to be content to write my mom and my twin sister.

CHAPTER 6

The train ride was pretty good. Milwaukee was the end of the line for us recruits on the train. We got off and boarded buses, which took us to the base. Once we got to the base, we exited the bus and the drill sergeant told all of us to stand in line. This was Great Lakes in February, the coldest time of the year in Michigan. It was so cold that the snot running down my nose froze before it reached the top of my lips. I had never felt such cold back home in Philadelphia. Being away from my hometown and my family was indeed a new experience. The drill sergeant marched us into the barracks where we were assigned bunks. The next morning we stood in line to go to the barbershop. After getting our crew cuts, we headed to the infirmary where we got shots to protect us from various diseases.

The next day, we got our uniforms and duffel bags. We then began our training as sailors. The training was harsh and intense. After about twelve weeks, we were given a twelve-hour liberty, and believe me we needed it. We were all cooped up together, going through intensive training and instruction for twelve weeks, and finally we could go to town and enjoy ourselves for twelve hours. When we returned to the base, we would have to assemble on a quarterdeck, and every one of us would have to report back individually. If anyone reported back drunk, the whole company would pay the price.

We kept this in mind, but we still went to town and did what we wanted to do. Restraining ourselves was very challenging, given all the time we had been cooped up in the barracks. We made a deal to check on each other to make sure we were all maintaining ourselves and not getting too drunk so that when we returned to the base we would all be in good standing. As our twelve hours of freedom dwindled, we checked on each other before returning to the base together. Then we all boarded a train for the base, reported back aboard, and returned to the barracks.

Soon we were back to the grind, back to our military training and to our schooling. Finally, after many grueling months in boot camp, it was time for our graduation. Some of us got to see family members who were able to attend. Since Great Lakes was so far away from Philadelphia, I knew my parents would not be able to come out. A lot of other guys weren't able to see their parents, but we still enjoyed our graduation. It was a very good day for everyone in my company.

CHAPTER 7

After the graduation exercises, we headed back to the barracks to get our orders for where we would report next. Would we go to Vietnam, or would we be assigned to a base or to a ship? We were all eager to learn what lay ahead. Some of us were ordered to ships, some of us to bases, and some of us to schools. No one had orders to go to Vietnam, thank God.

My recruiter had told me that my score on the entrance exam and my performance and grading at boot camp would help determine whether I got the type of job I wanted in the service. I wanted to get into the aviation field. My orders were to report to the Johnsville Naval Air Development Center (NADC) in Warminster, Pennsylvania. My rank would be airman recruit. I was very excited and pleased. My rank indicated I was in the aviation field, so I knew I would eventually be able to fly, something I had always wanted to do. I felt blessed by God to have gotten those orders.

I was not due to report to the base until Monday morning. However, I reported early on Friday morning and got settled into the barracks. Then I left for Philly to spend the weekend with my family and friends before returning to the base in uniform on Monday morning.

When I got home, my mother asked me about the training in boot camp, and as I explained what I had done there, I found myself using curse words. My mother immediately interrupted me and asked, "What are you saying? You know better than that. You were taught better than that. Where did you pick up that language?" I suddenly realized I had become a different person after going through boot camp. I had always believed in Christ, attended church every week, and prayed, but now my mother noticed a difference in me. I never stopped trusting and believing in the Lord, but I had picked up bad habits during my time in boot camp. I was cursing like a sailor, something I had never done before.

I spent time with the family while I was on leave, and I got back to church on Sunday. Everyone there was happy to see me. I was hoping to run into my ex-girlfriend, but unfortunately she wasn't in church. I didn't have her new phone number, so I wasn't able to get in touch with her. Fortunately, I had an alternative. I took a trip to Atlantic City to visit a woman I had met on the phone while I was at boot camp. She was a cousin of one of my navy buddies, and she had asked me to come see her in Atlantic City when I got out of boot camp.

CHAPTER 8

After visiting the woman in Atlantic City, I went to see a friend from school on Friday evening. It was probably ten-thirty or eleven at night when I left her. I was standing on a corner, eating an ice cream cone as I waited for the bus back to my mother's house. A police car drove by twice, and the officers looked at me. I felt uncomfortable. Finally, the third time they appeared, they stopped right in front of me. The cops sat in the car and kept looking at a picture and looking over at me. Then one of them got out of the car, walked over to me, and asked me my name. I gave him my name. Then he asked me what I was doing in the area. I said I was visiting a friend. He asked me to take them to my friend's house. "I'm not going to do that," I said. "It's late. It's almost midnight."

The cop told me I fit the description of someone who was raping women in the area, and the officers grabbed me and put me in the car. "Since you don't want to take us to your friend's house, we're taking you downtown," one of them said. As we headed downtown, I tried to reason with them. "I'm in the navy," I said. "I just came home on leave and I was visiting a friend. I don't know what you're talking about." I realized they weren't interested in anything I had to say. They showed me the picture, and one of them said, "This is you."

When I was shown the picture, I got scared because the person in that picture looked like me. However, he had a mustache, and I was clean shaven. When we entered the police station, the officers pushed me against a wall and told me to stand there and not to move. I got tired of standing, so I sat down. A sergeant grabbed me and shouted, "I said stand up. You don't sit down in here."

"Listen, guy," I said. "I'm not who you think I am. I'm in the navy and I'm stationed at NADC Warminster, Pennsylvania. Give them a call and they'll verify who I am." The officers continued to insist I was the rapist they were looking for until finally a lieutenant heard me asking them to check me out to verify my identity. When they called the base, it was late at night, and the duty officer said, "We don't have a Tom Dykes stationed here." When I protested, the duty officer checked again and said, "Oh, wait a minute. Yes, we do have a Tom Dykes. He just came on board early this morning, and he is stationed here at NADC Warminster. He is who he says he is." I was very relieved to hear that. Then the sergeant who had given me grief said, "You can leave."

"You guys brought me to this station, and I don't know where I am," I told him. I said the officers owed me transportation to the nearest subway or to another spot where I could get back home. So the lieutenant in charge told the sergeant to drive me to the subway and to put me on a train. I will never forget this frightening experience. When I recall the incident, I think of the many people who have been imprisoned for crimes they didn't do. I could have been one of them, but because God was watching over me that didn't happen.

My mom often told me, "There will always be misunderstanding between people. And a lot of times people will mistake you for someone else. Even the police will mistake you for somebody else." I believe each of us has an exact match somewhere. After this incident, I decided to buy a car so I could drive myself to and from the base without any problems.

The weekend was over and when I reached the base, I got orders from the duty officer to report to special services. I learned this was an area where sailors on the base would come for recreation. That was where I was sent to work. I was confused because I was an airman recruit and this area had nothing to do with aviation. I had to get to the bottom of this. The person who ran special services was a civilian, and the person under him was a second-class petty officer. I wanted to find out why I was put in special services when I should have been in the aviation department. I noticed there were almost no African Americans on the base, and I wondered what was going on. I asked to speak to the officer in charge of the special services division. The officer assured me he would check into the situation but said that in the meantime I would have to remain in special services. He promised he would get back to me as soon as possible. I worked in special services for about a month before I finally got a call to go talk to the division officer. The officer explained that there had been a mix-up in my paperwork and that I could move to the helicopter division the following month.

The weekend came and I was on my way to Philly to visit family and friends. I decided to purchase a car. I found one that I wanted, and it didn't cost much. It was a 1965 Chevy Corvair; it was a weird little car that had the engine in the back and the trunk in the front. There were a lot of little issues with the car, but I decide to buy it anyway. One issue was that the engine was known to catch on fire because the carburetors would overheat and leak fuel. This, of course, would cause the whole car to catch on fire. This was a cause for concern, but I didn't worry too much about it. I wanted to have transportation between the base and Philly, so I purchased the car.

On Sunday night I had a car and could now drive myself back to the base. The car performed well on its maiden voyage from Philadelphia to Warminster. I was still working in special services, but I had only about a week to go before I moved to the helicopter division. That would be my permanent position at the base. Once I got up to the helicopter division, I introduced myself to everyone there. To my amazement, there was only one African American sailor in the division. He was a second-class petty officer. He was pretty much ready to be transferred out or to retire. I often wonder if I was assigned to work in the helicopter division because of my last name. Whatever the reason, I was there, and I was going to make sure that whatever I did, I would be the best at it.

I was the only African American working in the hangar in the helicopter division. In fact, there were no more than three other African Americans on the base. I was a jet mechanic in the helicopter division. I was taught the many functions of a helicopter and learned its systems— the landing gear, the main rotor blades, the tail rotor, the transmission, the engines, the interior, and all the hydraulic systems. I made sure to get the tech manuals and absorbed all the information I could about the three types of helicopters we had in the division. I had the opportunity to work on all three, a challenging job. I worked from the ground up, striving to become a good jet mechanic. I stayed after hours at the end of the day, studying and working hard to prove myself. I promised myself that I would spend as much time as possible learning all I could about those helicopters, and I stuck with it.

I did troubleshooting to understand how each helicopter functioned. The helicopters were similar, but they had different functions. It was very important to learn the functions of each aircraft, so I spent extra time teaching myself all the aspects of these helicopters. I wanted to become a helicopter plane captain or crew chief, and to do that I had to know as much as possible about each aircraft. Once I passed the exams and was considered flight-worthy, I could fly on a helicopter. If there were a problem in the air, I would know how to solve it. I enjoyed my work. I wanted to get up in the sky, and now I had the perfect opportunity. I wasn't going to screw up and lose it, so I spent a great deal of time working on these helicopters and studying them inside and out.

On weekends, I didn't have duty, so I took a break from studying and went to Philly to see family and friends. Once the weekend was over, I headed back to the base in my '65 Chevy Corvair. I was driving up Route 611 on a Sunday evening when I stopped at a Dunkin' Donuts in Jenkintown for coffee and a doughnut. While I was sitting in the shop, a waitress said, "Oh, somebody's car is on fire out there." She called the fire department. When I looked out the window, I saw that my Corvair was engulfed in flames. There was nothing I could do. The fire department put out the fire, but the manager of the Dunkin' Donuts told me I had to get the car off of the lot. The police told me the same thing. I would have to call a tow company to remove the car and junk it. I called the closest tow company in the area. When the tow truck arrived, the driver told me what the job would cost. I said that I didn't have cash on me but that if he would take me to the base I could get the money from my locker.

The driver and a coworker hooked up the car. Then I got in the truck with the guys and they drove me to the base. I got the money from my locker, paid the driver, and that was the last I saw of my Corvair. I was once again without transportation. In time I asked my friends to let me know if anyone was interested in selling a car. Meanwhile, I continued working in the helicopter division, trying to learn what I needed to know about the helicopters. I would help other sailors in the division with preflight and postflight inspections and would assist in other inspections. I was also a wing walker. I would walk alongside of an aircraft as it was being towed from the hangar to the helicopter pad for takeoff, making sure the aircraft cleared the building or any other potential obstacle.

Sailors were assigned to divisions according to rank, and all were responsible for standing watch on the base night and day. We did this to make sure the base was secure. The hangar, the barracks, and the quarterdeck were in the interior of the base. The exterior of the base was secured by civilian personnel. I appreciated my position in the helicopter division. I felt especially good about it because I was one of very few African Americans on the base. The position made me feel very good about myself. The other African Americans on the base weren't assigned meaningful positions; most were doing cleanup jobs. One of these African Americans was the smallest guy in the navy. His congressman had helped him get in, but he didn't have any rank. He worked in a jet shop, but because of his size, he was assigned to go inside the jets' fuel tanks to clean them. I encouraged him several times to hit the books like I was doing and to work on taking the exam to earn a higher rank. I explained that rank had its privileges in the military. Unfortunately, his plans were from different from mine.

Seeking to be productive on the base, I decided to join the color guard. Its functions included hoisting the flag in the morning and taking it down in the evening. Members of the color guard attended military funerals when asked. We would provide military honors for the deceased and would present the family with a flag. One of my jobs was to blow taps on my trumpet at the military funerals. Whenever there was a funeral, we would be called to go. I was honored to perform this service.

I continued to gain mechanical experience as I worked in the helicopter division. One day the division's chief petty officer told me the division officer wanted to send me to school to learn more about the helicopters. They saw my performance and thought this would benefit the division and the base. I said this would be fantastic, and I accepted the offer. I prepared to go to school to study jet engines, reciprocating engines, airframes, and power plants and to gain the training I needed to continue working on aircraft. I became an airman recruit upon completing boot camp, and now I was an airman apprentice. I knew that once I finished school, I would rise in rank and become a petty officer one day. That was my goal. I thanked God that I had been blessed to receive so many good things.

My first class petty officer had heard I was looking for a car, and he told me he wanted to sell a 1965 Chevy Impala with a 283 engine. He asked if I was interested. I looked at the car after duty and liked it, so I gave him a down payment of $50. I told him I would give him the rest when he was finished painting the car. He was asking $500. That was a lot of money at the time, but having seen the condition of the car, I thought this was a good deal, so I agreed to that price.

We got paid twice a month, so I put money aside and in a month's time, I had enough saved to buy the car. One weekend I decided to take a bus to Philly and to enjoy myself. I had been staying on the base for several months to study up on the helicopters and had saved a lot of money. I'll never forget the Friday evening when I was preparing to go to the city. I kept my money in my locker; I had about $600. I had earmarked $500 for the car, and the additional $100 was supposed to last me until my next pay date. Before taking a shower, I asked one of the guys in the berthing area to keep an eye on my open locker. He said he would do that.

When I came out of the shower and entered the berthing area, I saw this guy running toward the parking lot. When I looked in my locker, I noticed my money was not where I had put it. I counted the money and $100 was missing. I called the master-at-arms, who called the gate guard and told him to stop the guy from leaving the base. At this point the guy was in his car, and he ignored the gate guard's signal to stop. He nearly ran over the guard as he fled the base. The master-at-arms reported this to the duty officer. The duty officer told the shore patrol to search the area in Philadelphia where this guy lived and to return him to the base. While he wasn't found that weekend, he reported back to the base on Monday morning and had to go to the captain's mess to address a charge of theft. The military does not tolerate theft, and I believe the captain gave that sailor some type of restriction.

The theft set me back a little bit, but it wasn't long before I was able to get the car. I got a very good deal. I couldn't wait to drive this beautiful car to Philly to show it off to my family and friends. I had no duty one weekend, so I headed for Philly in my car. I drove to Atlantic City. I came back to Philly and hung out with my buddies. One of my female friends introduced me to one of her friends, and in a few weeks we met again and started seeing each other regularly. We talked about our families, and I explained to her that I was in the navy but that I could leave the base nearly every day as long as I reported each morning. She told me she lived with her father. I would call her and would drive to New Jersey to visit her. She introduced me to her parents and the rest of her family, and we started to go out quite often. I told her I was going away to military school in California and might be gone for a few months.

CHAPTER 9

The time had come, and I headed out to the airport to get a flight for California. Once I arrived in California, I checked in at the navy base at Ream Field in Imperial Beach. I got set up in the barracks and collected the information I needed for classes, which started on Monday. We were taught everything about jet and reciprocating engines and their power plants and about the airframes of all aircraft and the fundamentals of flight. We were given the information we needed to know about all aircraft—the types of airplanes, the wings, the flaps, the landing gear, the engines, the fuel systems, the electrical systems, and the hydraulic systems. We were taught the functions of jet engines and of reciprocating engines; the two are completely different. We also learned the functions of helicopters. I worked on helicopters at my base, so this information was very useful to me. There was so much to learn, and this was so important to me that I wanted to absorb as much as I could. I knew what I learned would benefit me far into the future, and I felt blessed by God to have had the opportunity to get this training.

I continued with my studies for several months until it was time for the final test before graduation. I couldn't wait to return to my base in Warminster, Pennsylvania, and to apply all I had learned. I had wanted to enter the aviation field even before I joined the navy. Now I had finally reached my goal. Having finished classes in California, I thought back to the time when my division officer and chief petty officer had offered to send me to school so I could learn more about the airframes and the power plants of the aircraft I would be working on back in Warminster. I realized they had seen something in me. They understood that I was open to learning and to new experiences, and they thought it was worth taking the chance to send me to school. I showed them I had that interest, and I thank God for giving me that type of spirit. I was sure I would always be the best at whatever I did.

I got my orders, and I was happy to be heading back to Warminster. But when I opened the orders, I discovered I was being sent to another school, the one in a town outside of Memphis, Tennessee. At this school I would be trained in aircrew survival. I was curious to find out what I would be taught, and I was very grateful to be able to go to another school that would help me in the aviation field. I hopped on a plane in California and headed for Memphis. When I reached Memphis, I traveled to a base outside of Millington, Tennessee, got set up in the barracks, and prepared for my classes. On the weekend, I got a chance to see some of the sights in Memphis, which wasn't far away. I joined several other sailors and experienced the nightlife there, and we enjoyed being out on the town.

We started school Monday morning and began training in aircrew survival, learning the responsibilities of a crewman, a plane captain, a crew chief, and other officers. We were taught how to survive at sea after our plane or helicopter went down. We were also taught search and rescue just in case we were assigned to SAR, or sea air rescue. I felt blessed to take part in these classes, and I thanked God for another opportunity that he put before me.

One day in class we were told that the next day would be very exciting for all of us. We were ordered to report to the swim area. When I first checked into the base, I had heard rumors that we would have to jump into a swimming pool from a platform twenty or thirty feet above the pool. When we got to the swim area the next day, lo and behold, we saw a gigantic tower that rose way above the swimming pool. There was a set of stairs with a "One Way" sign pointing up. The instructor explained that we were to go up the steps, walk to the edge of the platform, and jump into the pool. He said the goal was to simulate jumping from the deck of a ship.

Once we were on the platform, we were instructed on the proper way to jump into the pool. When we entered the water, we were taught how to stay afloat by using our pants as a floatation device. We then learned other ways of surviving in the water. The class was intense, important, and informative. If I were stuck out in the ocean for any period of time, I would be in a life-or-death situation. This class was all about surviving. I thought the training was very good. I hoped I would never be trapped in the water, but if I were, I would know how to survive. I would also know how to rescue someone from the water. I thanked God for this training. Now I had new orders to return to my base in Warminster.

CHAPTER 10

I had now gone to two schools, one in California and one in Tennessee. I had learned a lot and was ready to put my training to work once I returned to my base in Warminster. I was blessed to be able to receive aviation training. I hope my story is an inspiration to young people. An African American born and raised in inner-city Philadelphia, who worked hard to make a difference, became a leader and not a follower. Back in Warminster, I continued to work on the CH53, the SH3A, and the HH2D helicopters, observing and learning as much as I could about each aircraft. They were similar in certain ways, but they had differences that I had to learn. So I continued my studies and my research. I would often stay in the hangar for hours after duty and read the tech manual on each helicopter. I would spend time on each aircraft, familiarizing myself with the parts and the functions. I worked every day with the other aviation mechanics, electrical mechanics, and hydraulic mechanics.

Recognizing my efforts, my chief petty officer asked me to take the exam for petty officer. I was still just an airman apprentice, and he wanted to see me become a petty officer third class. He said the test shouldn't be hard for me to pass, because I had been to school and had worked on aircraft and had good knowledge of all three types of helicopters. I studied the manuals every day in my free time, preparing to take the test for ADJ3, aviation jet mechanic third class. I enjoyed my job as a helicopter mechanic, but I knew I needed to gain rank. As a petty officer, I could become a crew chief on the helicopters. And as a crew chief, I could fly in the helicopter during test flights or on missions.

The crew chief's responsibility was to oversee inspections on the aircraft before and after flight.

I studied day and night and took the test for aviation jet mechanic third class. I was told the results would probably come in several weeks. The navy assigns new ranks only a few at a time, choosing from the top scorers. Those with lower scores would have to retake the test at another time. I was confident I had done well. As I awaited the results, I continued my duties as an airman apprentice. I worked with petty officers and with the other airmen in the helicopter division, assisting in aircraft inspections before and after flights. I helped to transport helicopters to the pad and to prepare them for flight. I also assisted in calendar inspections of the aircraft. A calendar inspection is an inspection done once an aircraft has reached a certain number of flight hours. These were some of my duties in the helicopter division. It was exciting and interesting work.

The schooling I had received was valuable. I gained a lot of information that I used once I got back to the base. In my spare time, I continued to familiarize myself with the functions of the helicopters even after taking the test for third class petty officer. I also continued to stand watches on the base and to carry out other duties. I also remained active in the color guard, attending funerals. And I continued to visit my girlfriend on the weekends. I would drive to Philly and then visit her in New Jersey, spending a whole weekend off the base. On the weekends when I had duty, I would study the tech manuals so I would be ready if I had to retake the test.

One day my division chief said he wanted me to become plane captain for the three helicopters. A plane captain was responsible for making sure an aircraft was towed out to the pad and was prepped for the flight. A plane captain would signal the pilot and the copilot that the area was clear before they started the engines. He would also signal the pilot and the copilot when the helicopter was landing, assuring them the landing area was safe. Since they could not see all around the aircraft, the plane captain had to be their eyes. I looked forward to being a plane captain, and I couldn't wait to find out if I passed the test and would be promoted to third class petty officer.

One weekend I visited my mother in Philly, and she told me one of my younger brothers had been shot by the police in a case of mistaken identity. He had been paralyzed from the waist down. I immediately recalled the time I was stabbed while working for the drugstore. I also remembered my mother telling us if we dressed like all the boys in the neighborhood, we could be mistaken for one of them or even for a gang member. So now my younger brother was in the hospital. He still had the bullet in him, but thank God, he was still alive.

I headed back to the base Sunday night to get ready for duty on Monday. The next morning I learned the exam results had been posted on the quarterdeck. The moment of truth had arrived, and I was nervous, so I took my time going up to the quarterdeck. When I got there, I looked at the results and saw my name. I was being promoted to ADJ3 third class petty officer, effective within days of that notice. I was very excited and couldn't wait to call my family and my girlfriend to tell them about my accomplishment. My chief, the other petty officers, and the rest of the helicopter division crew were happy that I was being promoted. They knew how hard I worked and how I continued to learn about the aircraft. Now I could move forward, but there was still much more to learn. I had more responsibilities and greater things to accomplish. A third class petty officer patch was added to all of my uniforms. I became a plane captain for the three helicopters in the division, and I did more work as a third class petty officer. I was given more responsibilities as an aviation jet mechanic third class. I was pleased with that, and I was up for the challenge. I felt blessed to become a third-class petty officer, and I thanked God for giving me the knowledge and understanding to obtain what I wanted.

After my aircrew survival training and the classes I had taken, I had no problem gaining flight status and taking the exam for my aircrew survival wings. After obtaining flight status, I became part of the helicopter division's flight crew. I was given a flight suit, a helmet, and all the gear I needed to fly. Now I could go up with the aircraft when they flew. My dream had finally come true. I had chalked up a major accomplishment. Before my first flight in a helicopter, I was instructed on all the things that had to be done before takeoff. I learned the procedures for flight operations and the information that had to be provided on a flight sheet. Then I was instructed on the responsibilities of a crew chief and a plane captain aboard the aircraft. I was expected to be another set of eyes for the pilot and the copilot while flying.

On my first day in the air, I went up with another crew chief who showed me what to look for and how to perform my duties on the aircraft. I also learned how to operate the aircraft's rescue hoist. I got paid extra money if I had at least four hours of flight time during the previous month. I would go with the HH2 or the SH3A helicopter whenever one of them flew. I would be a crew member and plane captain. If there were inspections or mechanical problems, neither helicopter would go up. I knew I needed at least four hours of flight time for the month to get paid, so several times I signed my name on a flight sheet and flew in any other aircraft that was going up.

My greatest passion was flying in the helicopters as crew chief/plane captain. I preferred this to flying in any other aircraft on the base. I loved doing overhauls on the jet engines and performing calendar inspections on the helicopters. What excited me most, though, was being a part of the test flight after a calendar inspection and an engine overhaul. I always said that you can't pull over on a cloud to fix a problem. Therefore you must do an overhaul or an inspection correctly before you fly an aircraft. This was the rule I had long observed: do it right the first time.

I was still working as a jet mechanic, and I continued to serve on the color guard, hoisting the flag in the morning and in the evening at the base and playing taps at military funerals. My plate was pretty full, but I enjoyed every bit of what I did. It had now been some time since I became a third class petty officer, and I decided to ask my girlfriend to marry me. We made plans, we talked to our parents, and we set a date. The year was 1972, and in February I had extended my enlistment by thirteen months. My original enlistment had been for two years. This was just an extension of my military time. I didn't reenlist or take the reenlistment bonus that was offered. I did the extension mainly because I wasn't quite sure whether I wanted to stay in the navy or to get out at some point in the future. I chose a thirteen-month extension for the time being.

CHAPTER 11

Our wedding took place on May 27, 1972. It was a magnificent day, the best day of my life. My best man was one of my closest friends from high school, and other navy friends were in my wedding party. The wedding was fantastic. After the ceremony my wife and I returned to our apartment in Cornwell Heights, Pennsylvania, not far from the base. After our honeymoon I returned to the base and to my military duties. I continued to fly whenever the helicopters went up for a mission. It could be testing the aircraft or testing something new on the aircraft, because the base was a naval air development center. Something new was always being developed for the aircraft while I worked in the helicopter division at Warminster, and these innovations had to be tested. I was once asked to be plane captain/crew chief when a helicopter was flown to Roosevelt Roads, Puerto Rico, for testing. I was supposed be there for several months or until the testing was completed. I felt blessed to be asked to participate in this program. I thank God for giving me the ability to do what I did in the military and for allowing me to show young guys and girls what they can do once they set their minds on a goal.

I prepared myself for deployment to Roosevelt Roads. I got all the things I needed for the trip and left with the crew for Puerto Rico the following week. Once we reached the base at Roosevelt Roads, we got settled in and were given a hangar where we could store our SH3A helicopter. I was accompanied by two other petty officers from my helicopter division, the aircraft's pilot and copilot, and several civilian engineers who would be doing the testing on board the helicopter. The other two petty officers and I elected to live off base, and we found a hotel a few miles away. We could step out of the hotel and walk fifty to sixty feet to the beach. We enjoyed going to the beach when we were not flying. We flew twice a day, doing our testing for two to three hours in the morning and in the afternoon. Each time, we would fly over or near almost all of the Virgin Islands. I was very excited about what I was doing, and I stopped to think about a young kid from the inner city who never imagined himself being in a helicopter in the military, let alone seeing the Virgin Islands. I thought about how my twin sister and I used to call ourselves explorers. At this point I could say I was indeed an explorer.

In the late afternoon, we would go back to our hotel, relax on the beach, and spend time in the water. In the evening, we would drive to a nearby town, eat out, and enjoy ourselves. On the weekends when we were free, we would visit the El Yunque rain forest. We would also visit Old San Juan and would hit the casinos in Fajardo, where we had plenty of fun. One afternoon after we returned to the hotel, the owner of the restaurant invited me and the other two petty officers to his house for dinner that Friday evening. He told us to be prepared for a big dinner and not to eat much during the day. We went to his house Friday night and enjoyed the many dishes that his wife served. We were all full and couldn't eat any more. The next day when we returned to the hotel after flying, the owner of the restaurant told us his wife was very disappointed. We asked why, and he explained that when a woman in Puerto Rico cooks a meal, she expects everything to be eaten. We weren't aware of that custom. So he invited us again on the following weekend. This time he and his wife were pleased with our appetites.

We tested the aircraft for several months. When we completed the tests according to the specifications of the engineers, we prepared for the long journey back home to Pennsylvania. As the jet mechanic in charge, I would do a complete preflight inspection of the aircraft. All of the engineers and one of the petty officers had already headed home. The other petty officer and I would join the pilot and the copilot on the helicopter. The day before our scheduled departure, we had all our equipment and clothing on board and were ready to leave. Doing a final test, I tried to start the engines. Neither one responded, so I did some troubleshooting. I tried everything without success. I had the petty officer, who was an electrician, check things out, and still we could find no reason the engines would not start. We informed the pilot and the copilot that we were unable to get the engines started even after hours of intense electrical and mechanical work. The pilots told us to take a break and to start fresh the next day.

The petty officer and I resumed our efforts the next day and were able to get one engine started. That was a good sign. We worked feverishly until the end of the day but could not get the other engine started. Though I was just a third class petty officer, I had been selected to make this trip because of my aviation experience. My superiors also knew that I worked hard to solve any problem and that I wasn't a quitter. All of the troubleshooting we had done on the engine had failed, so we decided to call one of the bases back home and have an engine shipped to Puerto Rico. We would then install the new engine in our aircraft so we could fly our helicopter back home. The engine didn't arrive until about a week later, and once we got the thing, we were eager to install it. When we had done that, we fired up the engine, and everything worked fine. Both engines were running at 100 percent, and we were very happy that we could soon head home to Warminster.

I thanked God for giving me the knowledge and the experience to perform the emergency engine replacement. I was also grateful for the extensive aviation training I had received. Now I was able to apply what I had been taught. The pilots were pleased with my accomplishment. On the morning of our departure, we went to the operations office and filed our flight plan. I did an extensive preflight inspection of the aircraft and confirmed everything was operating at 100 percent. The pilot and copilot were pleased and were eager to get the helicopter up in the air. It felt good to finally be heading home after being away from our families for several months. We departed Puerto Rico and stopped briefly at Grand Turk Island to check the fluid levels, the engines, and the transmission. This was my responsibility as the jet mechanic and crew chief. I told the pilots that everything was fine and that we could continue our flight to Miami, Florida. The trip from Grand Turk Island to Miami took quite a few hours. As we neared Miami, the pilot radioed the Opa-locka coast guard station for our final approach pattern. I looked out the window as we flew along the Florida coast. The sandy beaches and the skyline of multicolored buildings were especially beautiful.

After hugging the coastline for several miles, we flew inland and landed at the Opa-locka coast guard station. We taxied to the parking area, shut down the aircraft, and got out. I kissed the ground. All of us were happy to be in Miami and closer to home. We were blessed that the weather was good and that we had no issues with the aircraft during the flight. We decided to stay in Opa-locka for a few days to relax after the long flight from Puerto Rico. I prayed God would continue to keep us safe when we left Miami and headed home to Warminster. After resting up for a few days, we went to the operations office and filed our flight plan for the trip home. I did a preflight inspection of the aircraft. We fueled up the aircraft and got it ready for departure.

On the way back to Warminster, both pilots said they wanted to put me in for a commendation for troubleshooting the aircraft, for ensuring that the engine was replaced in a timely manner, and for spending extra time making certain that the aircraft was safe to fly. I told the pilots I was just doing my job as an aviation jet mechanic and as a crew chief and plane captain. Nearing the Pennsylvania area, we radioed Warminster only to learn that flight operations at the base were shut down for the night. We had to land at Willow Grove Naval Air Base, which was several miles from Warminster. After landing, we got our gear and both pilots again thanked me for all the work I had done to ensure our safe trip home.

I stayed with the aircraft and did a postflight inspection, buttoned up the helicopter, and headed for the operations office where I called my wife to say that I was back and that she could meet me at the base in Warminster. Within the hour, my wife picked me up, and what a beautiful thing it was to see her again after several months. She was just as happy to see me. We missed each other after being apart for such a long time. But duty called for me to be wherever I had to be and to perform my job at 100 percent no matter what. The next day I drove back to the base and returned to the helicopter division. My chief, my division officer, the other petty officers, and the division crew were happy to see me, and they all congratulated me for getting the helicopter back safely. They were surprised that we were able to replace the engine in Puerto Rico. Everybody thanked me, and I felt very good about that. After speaking to everyone in the division, I drove over to Willow

Grove with the two pilots and a few other people to get the helicopter ready and to fly it back to Warminster.

I was glad to be back at the base and to resume my job as a jet mechanic on the helicopters. I was happy to be back to continue my duties as a color guard. And most important, I was happy and excited to be back for the birth of my first child. My wife had been pregnant for a while and was getting close to her due date. I would work at the base and would rush home every day after duty to be with my wife. Finally, as I was flying one day, we got a call from the base telling us to return because my wife was going into labor. I had to get her to the hospital so she could deliver the baby. We flew the chopper back to the base, and I got off and ran to my car. My wife and I got to the hospital, and a doctor checked her out and sent us home because she definitely was not ready. Since this was our first child, we didn't know what to expect, and the doctor explained that sometimes a woman would get a false alarm. He said a woman would know when it was time for her to go into labor. We returned home, and I made my wife as comfortable as possible. Later she told me she was ready, so we headed to the hospital again. A doctor checked her out, and yes, she was in labor.

I stayed at the hospital for hours, but it seemed like days because my wife was continually in labor. It was approximately seventeen hours before she finally delivered, and when the time came, I was there to help. I thanked God for blessing us with a healthy girl. Soon after, my wife returned home with our little daughter. Her family and my family came to see our little girl. When I returned to the base for duty, everyone congratulated me on the birth of my daughter. I resumed my duties with the helicopter division and with the color guard, and everything was back to normal. I thanked God for my blessings. I was blessed to be stationed near my wife and my daughter and to be able to return to them at the end of the day. Other people in the military were far away from their loved ones. Some men were fighting in Vietnam; many had been away from their families for a long time. It's a lonely feeling to be separated from loved ones. I thank God every day for allowing me to be close to my family while I was serving in the military.

It had been weeks since I had returned from my deployment to Puerto Rico. One day when I entered the shop in my division, the chief petty officer pulled me aside to congratulate me. I was confused. I reminded him that he had already congratulated me on the birth of my daughter, but he said this was about something else. "The pilots you flew with in Puerto Rico put you in for a commendation," he said. They had nominated me as Sailor of the Quarter because of my outstanding performance on the engine installation and because of all the hard work I did while troubleshooting to correct the problem with the helicopter engines. "You spent countless hours troubleshooting until finally you had another engine sent to Puerto Rico, and you along with a couple of other petty officers installed that engine, tested it, and made sure the aircraft was ready for flight," the chief petty officer said. I told him I was just doing the job I was trained to do as an aviation jet mechanic. I felt God had blessed me with that knowledge. I troubleshot the problems, and everybody made it home safely.

CHAPTER 12

I never expected to be recommended for a commendation and to be recognized for my outstanding achievements. I was also surprised to learn that my picture would be taken and posted on the quarterdeck along with photos of other sailors on the base who had gotten recognition for outstanding performance. Within a few days, the photographer at the base took pictures of me and got information about where I lived and about my wife and my daughter. He told me my picture and the information I supplied would appear in a local newspaper. In September 1973 I received a plaque from the Southeastern Pennsylvania Council of the Navy League of the United States. The base commander presented the plaque at a ceremony held for me on the base.

Along with the plaque I received several other items and a trip with a P-3 Orion crew to several countries in Europe. I saw this award as another blessing from God. I had always wanted to fly and had done that and had been a plane captain on several helicopters. I had visited Puerto Rico when we did testing there, and now I had a free trip to Europe. The P-3 Orion was a hurricane hunter and would enter the eye of a hurricane to collect data. I was fortunate to go along with the crew to Europe. Though the crew was on official military business, I was just along for the ride. The navy gave me money to spend, and so I could enjoy myself in each place we visited.

Most important, I realized I was the first and perhaps the only African American sailor stationed at the Warminster base to be named Sailor of the Quarter. That accomplishment meant a great deal to me. I don't know if there were others after me, but I knew I was the first because I looked at the pictures of award recipients posted on the quarterdeck and never saw one of an African American. I was blessed to have been awarded for my accomplishments, and I thank God for that every day. Before receiving the award, I extended my enlistment by thirteen months for the second time. I continued to work as a mechanic in the helicopter division, to fly whenever necessary to maintain my flight status, to perform my color guard duties, and to stand watch on the base. I eagerly awaited my departure for Europe.

My days were full. I worked at least eight hours a day, and at the end of each day, I went home to my wife and daughter and spent the evening with them. In the morning, I returned to duty on the base. On weekends we would travel to New Jersey to see my wife's parents and would visit my family and friends in Philadelphia. Finally, after arriving at the base one Monday morning, I learned that my trip was coming up soon. I was instructed to go for a briefing on information I would need. I wanted to find out what I needed to take with me and what my duties would be. I was instructed to do nothing but simply to enjoy myself in the countries we visited. Those countries were Spain, Italy, and Portugal. I was very excited. I couldn't wait to tell my family about the places I was going to see. I couldn't wait to see how people live in other countries. I was a young African American, born and raised in inner-city Philadelphia. I had become an aviation jet mechanic and a crew chief on two helicopters. I had been named Sailor of the Quarter at my base and believed I was the first African American to have received that honor there. I felt blessed to have gotten that honor and to be able to travel abroad with the P3 crew. I learned that the P-3 would be departing Warminster for Europe in a few days. Our first stop would be in Spain, and from Spain, we would fly to Italy and then to Portugal. We would spend time in each of these places while the high-ranking officers took care of military business.

After we had been briefed on what to expect in these countries, I returned home and explained everything to my wife. I packed and prepared myself for this long trip. I was still amazed that this was happening. What were the chances that a young African American born in inner-city Philadelphia would be traveling to Europe to visit countries like Italy, Spain, and Portugal? I was very grateful. My twin sister and I used to call ourselves the explorers. And now I was exploring again, but this time, I was headed for a different part of the world. And I would be able to share this experience with my family and friends.

Finally, the departure day arrived. That morning, I kissed my wife and my daughter goodbye and headed for the base. When I got there, I loaded all my gear onto the P-3 and got comfortable. When I boarded the plane, all the crew members were happy to see me. They were just as excited as I was. This was my first time on board a P-3 Orion, and I was about to take a trip to Europe. Everyone—the captain, the copilot, the engineer, and the crew—told me to sit back and relax because it was going to be a long ride—ten to twelve hours to our first destination, Spain.

The P-3 Orion was very comfortable compared with other planes I had flown in. At Warminster, I would fly just to get my hours in for the month. I flew in an S-2, a C-117, the C121 Constellation, and other aircraft on the base. The Constellation provided a fairly smooth ride, but flying on most of those aircraft was rough going. The P-3 Orion had many functions, and it flew pretty smoothly. We had a serene flight, and I got first-class treatment from the crew. I was very impressed. Flying over the Atlantic Ocean at that time of the year was exciting. Looking down at the Atlantic, I could see icebergs that looked like little white dots. That's how high up we were. The ocean was a beautiful sight. After eleven or twelve hours, we were not far from Spain. We were to land at the base in Rota, Spain, in fifteen to twenty minutes. The seats in the P-3 Orion were comfortable—nothing like being crunched up in a seat on a commercial airliner with your knees in agony. When I left that airplane after the long flight, I felt pretty good, and I was happy to be on solid ground again.

Once we landed in Rota, the pilots got their gear and went to the flight operations office to take care of the paperwork. The crew members did a postflight inspection of the aircraft. Once they were finished, we left the base for a hotel. Our stay in Rota was brief, two or three days. We visited nightclubs, enjoyed the food, and mingled with other people. I wanted to see a bullfight, but we didn't get the chance. We soon departed Spain for Naples, Italy. I was very excited about seeing these countries. I felt blessed to have an opportunity I might never have again. I was thankful for my accomplishments as an aviation mechanic. And I was thankful to the pilots who had recommended me for an award for my outstanding work in Puerto Rico. I thanked God for making all of this possible.

Our business in Rota was finished, and we were moving on to Naples. I had such a good time in Rota that I didn't want to leave. Some of the crew members told me that Rota was a good place to visit but that Naples and Portugal were just as nice. Most of the crew had been to these places in the past. They knew where and where not to go, so I was sure they would take me to the best spots and show me sights I would probably never see again. In the morning, we boarded the P-3 and headed for Naples. I was told that the trip was about 1,200 miles. We wouldn't be in the air too long, and that was a good thing. I got comfortable in my seat, looked out the window, and enjoyed the beautiful view. We took off, gained altitude, and before long were on our final approach to the air base in Naples. We landed, gathered our baggage, and exited the aircraft. I waited in the base operation office until the crew finished the postflight inspection. Then we left the base and headed to a hotel in Naples.

The hotel was beautiful, and the view from my suite overlooking the city was wonderful. I was intrigued by the many designs and colors of the surrounding buildings and by the busy streets. We were fortunate to have spacious private rooms. The linen was fine, and the bedding was comfortable. The walls in my suite were decorated with lovely paintings of Naples and of other places in Italy. We had everything we needed in our rooms, and we had access to a balcony from which we could see different areas of the city. And it was beautiful. I was grateful to have been given money to pay for my hotel stays and my meals. I had plenty to spend, and I was going to enjoy myself in Naples. I looked forward to dining out and to tasting Italian food. I also considered going to Rome to see the Coliseum, something everyone wants to see in that city.

On our first night in Naples, we all went out to dinner and enjoyed the food. While we were at the restaurant, we were approached by a tour guide who said he would be more than happy to show us around Naples. We agreed to do that, so the next day we met up with the tour guide. He showed us historical sites and took us to an outdoor café where we could sit down and eat. We ordered pizza and discovered the pizza in

Italy is much different from the pizza in the United States. We sat in the café enjoying pizza and wine and taking in the sights. Our guide said he wanted us to see the nightlife in Naples. He also showed us the places to avoid in Naples. We enjoyed going from club to club. The next day we got together with our guide again and picked up where we had left off the previous day. Our guide showed us some historical sites in Naples that we had not seen. We ate at new places and enjoyed the food. We had wanted to go to Rome to see the Coliseum and the Vatican, but earlier that day our chief petty officer had said we would be leaving Italy the following day for Lajos Field in Portugal. Led by our tour guide, we saw as much of Naples as we could see into the evening. Then we went out to clubs and had a good time on our last night in Naples, even though we were disappointed at being unable to see Rome.

The next morning we departed Italy and headed to Portugal. Throughout the trip, I felt like a guardian angel was watching over all of us, keeping us out of harm's way. I thanked God for that because anything could have happened to us, but we were protected during our time in Spain and Italy. As we traveled through Europe, I prayed to God to keep us safe and to bring us home unharmed. The trip to Portugal didn't take much time, and we were told our stay would be brief, no more than two days. We had time to recuperate from our travels in Spain and Italy and to prepare for the trip back to the United States. We checked into the housing unit set aside for our stay in Portugal. Lajos Field was busy around the clock, with aircraft coming in day and night. The meals were excellent, and we could eat at any time of the day because the mess hall was open twenty-four hours. We relaxed and counted the time until we boarded our P-3. All of us were ready to go home. I enjoyed my stay in Spain—the sightseeing, the history, the food, and the drinks. I was intrigued by the lifestyle of the Spanish people. I also enjoyed Italy—the lifestyle, the food, the entertainment, and the historical sites.

The lifestyle in the countries we visited was much different from ours. The time had finally come, and we were told we would be departing Portugal in the morning. The experience I had abroad was something to remember, and I thank God for allowing me to see how people live in other parts of the world. I am grateful for what we have in the United

States. We are so blessed to have the freedom to move about, to do what we want to do, and to eat what we want. People elsewhere live much differently than we do here, and we take so much for granted. We Americans have plenty, but some of us are still not satisfied. I thank God for being an American and for being able to live, to worship, and to come and go as I please.

CHAPTER 13

We boarded the aircraft, and soon we were on our way back to the United States. Finally, after many hours in the air, we were just minutes away from Warminster. I looked out the window of the aircraft and saw our base. It was a beautiful sight. We had not seen our families in quite a while, and now we were finally home, safe and sound. I was happy to be back with my wife and my daughter. Since I had been away so long, I decided to stay home with them that weekend. Returning to the base on Monday, I got right back into the rhythm of things; it was like I had never left. One of the helicopters was due for inspection, and I had to speed up the process, so I got busy. Lunchtime came, and I headed down to the mess hall and saw a lot of the guys I hadn't seen in a long time. Even the cooks were happy to see me. The base was like a big family. We all knew each other, and we loved and respected each other for who we were. Many of us flew together, and some of us worked together after hours off base.

I was constantly blessed by God with jobs after duty that allowed me to make extra money to provide for my family. Though I finally gave up working those jobs, I had saved a considerable amount of money from my earnings. Now I was several months away from the end of my second thirteen-month extension in the navy, and that was the last extension I could do. I would have to decide whether to reenlist for an additional four or six years with a reenlistment bonus or to leave the navy at the end of my extension period in a few months. This would be a hard decision to make. I loved my job as a jet mechanic, and I was contemplating taking the exam for petty officer second class. I loved flying and I loved the travel, but I wasn't quite sure if that was good for me and my family. I thought about the times I was at school and was away from my family. I also thought about the time I traveled in Europe, and I looked at other people's situations when they had been away from their families. I had seen and heard of several divorces in the military. I also wondered where my orders might take me after reenlistment.

I gave the question a lot of thought. I talked with my wife, and she was fine with whatever I wanted. I finally decided to end my enlistment when my second extension in the navy was up. As the time drew closer, I recalled going to the recruiting office to sign up for the navy. I went back to my time in junior high school, to all of my encounters, to all of things I was taught in carpentry and cabinetmaking class. I thought about myself as a young boy and about the responsibilities my siblings and I had at home. I remembered my first job and the values our parents instilled in us. My father and my mother were there for us all the time. My mother kept us in church. She was a praying mother, and she asked God to protect us in every situation. My siblings and I all went to church. We enjoyed church, Sunday school, and Bible study. As we got older, we tended to go our separate ways. Some of us strayed from church, but we all remembered what was instilled in us by our parents and what we were taught in church, in Bible study, and in Sunday school. And we all knew what the Bible says. We knew God had protected us through chaos, tribulations, and all of life's other experiences.

I've been blessed many times. God has watched over me and has kept me out of harm's way. He guarded me during boot camp and at the schools I attended. He protected me when I flew as a plane captain on three helicopters and on every other flight I took. God kept me safe during the testing operation in Puerto Rico, the long journey from Puerto Rico to Miami, and the trip from Miami back to Warminster. That's why I believe in God; only he could have protected me. And even though my wife went through seventeen hours of labor, God gave us a healthy daughter. I give all of the honor and glory to God. I trust him and believe he is a provider. I decided to exit the navy and to let God lead me where I should go. I knew I would survive if I continued to trust him. I looked forward to leaving the navy and to starting the next phase of my life. However, I wouldn't know what that next phase might involve until I exited the military.

Time flew by, and suddenly only a few days remained before my departure from the navy. I got everything in order and took care of all my exit exams. I also turned in my flight gear and anything else I had used on the base. Meanwhile, I continued to do my flying and to work in the helicopter division. My shipmates were disappointed to learn I was not going to reenlist. My division officer and a chief petty officer in the helicopter division were saddened to find out I was leaving the navy. They had enjoyed working with me. They had enjoyed my company, and they had respected my professionalism. They had appreciated my work ethic, and they told me this was something they would miss. I was happy in a way to be getting out of the navy, because I knew I would be able to spend a lot more time with my wife and my daughter. I would no longer have to go away on a mission and leave them behind. I thought about that. I also thought about the good times I'd had in Warminster. I thought about all of the friends I had made, and I knew I would miss every one of those guys. But the day had finally come.

CHAPTER 14

February 1, 1974, was my last day in the United States Navy and my last day at the naval air development center in Warminster, where I had served for four years. This was a wonderful day for me. I was happy to become a civilian. I was also thankful to God for blessing me and for keeping me safe throughout my time in the navy. I would spend the rest of my life as a civilian, but I would never forget my time in the navy and all the wonderful people I knew during those years. The good times, the bad times, all my experiences and encounters, would remain in my memory. But on that beautiful Friday morning, I could think only about the fact that I was now a civilian.

I was ready to reenter the workforce, and I took into account my experience as a jet mechanic in the navy and as a carpenter and a cabinetmaker in high school. Then I remembered the company in Glenside, Pennsylvania, where I had worked before entering the navy. I remembered the owner telling me that when I left the navy my job would still be available. I called the company and identified myself. The person I spoke with was happy to hear from me and said my job was indeed still available if I wanted it. The only problem was that the company had moved to South Carolina, and I wasn't about to move there. I thanked the company for offering me my job back but politely declined.

I continued to look for jobs in the Bucks County area where my family was living. I was fortunate to land a job at a packing company not far from our home. I was very happy to get work only a few days after leaving the military. I thanked God for my new job. The place was quite busy. I worked five days a week and got plenty of overtime.

Sometimes the overtime was mandatory because of the demand for the company's product. I felt pretty good about the overtime because I made a lot of money, and I got accustomed to it. My goal was to put away enough money so we could move from our apartment in Bucks County and perhaps buy a home in New Jersey. I took all of the opportunities for overtime presented to me. My wife understood, and I did this for quite some time. During my time at the packaging company I made a lot of new friends. These were people I worked with every day, and we had a good relationship with one another and even with the foreman.

The job was very intense and the place was very noisy. The printing on the cartons was done on a printing press that was probably about a block long. Humongous rolls of cardboard were fed into the machine, which was computer-programmed. The company had just purchased this new printing press from France. Since the company's employees did not speak French, the company had to hire French operators for the machine. They were familiar with the printing press and would instruct the workers on how to operate it. Still, there were constant printing errors and problems with the font sizes, and the colors weren't right. It took some time, but the workers were finally able to run the press without problems. At that point the company was able to send the French operators back home. It was very important for the workers to learn the operation of the press, because this machine cost the company a lot of money. The press was very efficient and very fast, and I guess it was well worth the money. Once all the bugs had been worked out, the printing press operated twenty-four hours a day, seven days a week. I worked twelve hours a day maybe every other day, and some weekends. The overtime continued for months. I thank God for keeping me out of harm's way when I worked for that company.

I realized after a while that I was spending too much time working and very little time at home with my wife and daughter. I started to burn out. With all the overtime, I wasn't getting the sleep I needed. I wasn't eating, and my resistance was going down. I started getting sick, and I decided to cut back on the overtime and to spend more time with my family. I thought of my years in the military when I was away from my wife and my daughter. But I was government property then, and I had no choice about when I would be home. I had to follow orders. But now I was a civilian, and I did have control over when I would be home. I realized I shouldn't let a job determine how much time I spent with my family. Though the plant was noisy, work conditions weren't that bad, and I liked my job. But I knew something had to change. I had to spend more time with my wife and my child. I was an excellent worker and had a good relationship with my foreman and my coworkers. I was well respected and was always available to help out new employees. I spoke to my foreman, and he was okay with me decreasing my overtime hours. I appreciated that. When you put yourself in a good position and you become a respectable person, it pays off in the long run. That was something I was always taught as a kid. Now I was able to spend more time with my wife and my daughter. On the weekends and even after work, we would travel to Philly and to New Jersey to visit our parents. We had plenty of time to look for a house in New Jersey.

CHAPTER 15

We finally found a nice place in South Jersey. It was a two-story house, just the right size for us. We decided to check it out to see if that was what we wanted. We looked at the area and checked the price. It was affordable. We were newlyweds with one child, and now we were going to be homeowners. We were very excited about that. We were also excited about moving from Bucks County to a very nice area of New Jersey. My weekends were now free, so I had time to go to New Jersey to finish up the last details on the purchase of the house. After starting my job at the packaging company, I bought a brand-new 1973 Chevelle Malibu. The car I had while in the navy was the 1965 Chevy Impala I bought from a petty officer when I was stationed in Warminster. The money I received from selling the Impala went toward our relocation to New Jersey.

We reached an agreement on the house, and it was now just a matter of time before we moved all our belongings from the apartment in Bucks County to New Jersey. We were blessed again because the military provided a moving company for us. I would travel back and forth from New Jersey to the packaging company in Bucks County until I found a job in New Jersey, and that wasn't too hard. I've always had pretty good luck in securing jobs. My wife and I now owned our first house. My family and her family were amazed at how quickly we had moved from the apartment to the house. I did not want to use my VA benefits for the purchase, because I wasn't sure if this would be the last home we would buy. However, I did plan to use other VA benefits such as education aid. I got a job in New Jersey so I wouldn't have to commute back and forth to Pennsylvania, and we finally moved into our new home.

We found everything exactly as we wanted it. The furniture had been put in place, and the bedrooms had been set up. My daughter's bed was in her room. We settled in, and I was grateful to God that we were able to make the move and to find a house. I started my new job working in a cabinet shop and happened to be the only African American employee. When I began work, the owner walked me through the shop and explained the machinery used to make the items produced there. He introduced me to the other workers and showed me the procedures for making the furniture, cabinets, and countertops manufactured at the shop. I was grateful to get this job and thankful for the useful information.

I was familiar with this operation because I had learned most of this stuff in my high school carpentry and cabinetmaking class and in working with my shop teacher on weekends. I was very excited about helping to manufacture the items the shop sold. I was to work with a person who would show me the procedures for making kitchen and bathroom countertops and for cutting the laminate for the tops. He would also show me how to glue the countertops and the laminate. I had never had the opportunity to make a countertop. I had not learned to do this in my high school carpentry class or when I worked with my shop teacher. He manufactured the countertops we installed when we did remodeling, and I never worked with him to see how the countertops were made and how to laminate them. This was a first for me, so I found the operation interesting. I learned quite a few things that first day.

I felt blessed to have a job near my new home and to do something I loved—working with wood. I loved my job at the cabinet shop. As the months passed, the owner saw my progress and gave me good assignments, handing me blueprints for furniture. He noticed that I was familiar with the layout and the operation of the shop and with all the machinery. I got along with everyone and felt blessed by God to be in a place that was like a nice little family. Everyone worked cooperatively. I was also thankful that God had blessed me with this job so quickly. Each time I left a job, by the grace of God, I soon landed another one. I thanked God for all his blessings from high school, to my first job after graduation, to my time in the military, to my first job after leaving the military, to my latest job. I had never even applied for unemployment. God has blessed me so much, and I must continue to talk about that because if it wasn't for the grace of God throughout my life, where would I be?

Besides manufacturing items in the cabinet shop, I sometimes went out to install them. I felt very good about my job, but again I found myself in a situation where I was the only African American working in a small company. That was true of several jobs I had in high school. Then I joined the navy. I was the first African American male stationed at the base in Warminster and the first named Sailor of the Quarter there. Wherever I've worked, I've always wanted to make a difference and to be a leader and not a follower. I like to talk about this and to encourage people by showing how an African American who was born and raised in inner-city Philadelphia achieved so much. Everyone is capable of great achievements, but the first step is to set a goal. I've been through a lot, I've I seen a lot, and I've always had the will to make a difference. I was raised with a mother and a father at home. My siblings and I were taught good values. Regardless of how we were raised, we all grow up, we all have our own minds, and we all have our own destinies. I believe my destiny was to explain my life to other people. Perhaps that will make a difference to someone else.

I continued working in the cabinet shop, manufacturing products and installing them in homes and businesses. I loved my job, and my wife liked having me work close to home. However, close to a year after I started working there, a fire destroyed most of the cabinet shop and the company shut down. I found myself out of work. I had good times at the cabinet shop and good people to work with, and it was all over in one night. I prayed to God for a new job.

I didn't give up. I just rolled up my sleeves and the pavement, looking for another job. Finally, a friend mentioned that the company where he worked was always hiring and that the place paid well. I filled out an application there, and lo and behold God was with me again, blessing me with another job. The company was in Pennsauken, New Jersey, and manufactured pharmaceutical items such as caps for test tubes and rubber needle covers. I was hired to operate the molds where we put the rubber to make the needle covers and the test tube caps. The molds had to go into big presses. The press would close, squeeze the rubber in the mold, and form the shapes we were looking for. That area of the shop was very hot because the temperature of the molds and of the presses was maybe five hundred degrees. Some of the molds were even hotter. It took me some time to get used to the operation. I had to run five or six presses, and everything had to be done in a certain amount of time. Within two weeks I had everything down pat, as if I'd been doing the job for years. The guy who worked across from me was very impressed by how quickly I caught on to the operation. And I started to like the job. The plant was awfully hot, but I got used to it. This was different from the cabinet shop. I was able to learn new skills while working in this factory. I acquired new friends among my coworkers, and we all got along very well.

I had now been out of the navy for about two years, and my daughter was almost two years old. That was about as long as we had been living in our house, and we decided it wasn't quite what we wanted. Cars were parked on both sides of our small street. One morning during our first year there, I left the house to go to work and found the driver's door on my brand-new Chevelle Malibu smashed in. I was upset because someone had sideswiped my car and none of my neighbors had told me who did it. After asking several of them, I finally found out that a woman who lived on our street was a poor driver and had sideswiped other neighbors' cars in the past. But this didn't prove she had done it, so I couldn't accuse her of damaging my car. I reported the damage to my insurance company and had the problem fixed.

Given the parking problem and other issues I had with the house, my wife and I agreed we were going to sell it, move back into an apartment, and save money to buy a house elsewhere in South Jersey. That was our game plan. We knew we didn't have much equity in the house, and we knew we wouldn't get much for it, but we chose to take our losses. We decided to contact a real estate agent and put the house on the market. I continued working at the factory as a mold operator. I enjoyed my job, but I was working the night shift, which meant I wasn't home at night with my wife and my daughter. But my wife and I knew that the money was good, and we accepted the situation. The extra pay I got for being on the third shift worked out very well for us.

CHAPTER 16

A month after we put our house up for sale, the real estate agent contacted us to say that quite a few people were interested in buying the place and would have no problem securing a loan to make the purchase. With that reassurance, my wife and I put in applications at apartments in South Jersey, not too far from where I was working. We wanted to be prepared just in case we reached a quick agreement on the sale. We were eager to sell and to move into an apartment. Then we could save money to buy a much better house. I had a feeling we would soon have a buyer for our house and would be able to move into an apartment that was comfortable and affordable. Finally, after several more weeks, the real estate agent told us we had a buyer who had been approved for a loan to purchase the property. There was joy in our hearts. We had arranged to rent a suburban apartment. So days after learning we had a buyer for the property, my wife and I packed our things and prepared for our big move. The sale would be finalized after the house was inspected. The down payment on the apartment was a lot less than I thought it would be. I got a discount because I was a veteran. It was very good of the apartment managers to do that. I was again blessed.

Earlier in the year I had enrolled in a course on architectural drafting. I had looked into studying this while I was in my high school carpentry and cabinetmaking class, and it was always something I wanted to do. Drafting was a part of the trade, so I thought I should learn more about making architectural blueprints and reading them. I got my work hours changed to the day so I could go to the drafting class in the evening. I was blessed by God to be able to do this. I had a passion for knowledge of the architectural trade. I had so much to learn, and I wanted to get all of the training and schooling I could. With my veterans benefits, I was able to get additional schooling, and I took advantage of that. My parents taught me that I could never learn too much and that when the opportunity arose, I should take advantage of it and get as much schooling as possible. Finally, the time had come for the closing on the house. The closing went well, and now we had to pack up and move into the apartment. This was special for me, my wife, and my daughter.

We could do no better than break even on the sale of the house because we didn't have enough equity in it. My wife and I were happy to be out of the house and moving into an apartment where we could save our money to buy a larger house in a better area. We had plenty of help, so it took us just a few hours to move into the apartment. Once we were settled, we introduced ourselves to the neighbors on either side of us and upstairs from where we lived. The factory was about forty-five minutes to an hour from the apartment, and so was the school where I was taking the drafting class. But that was fine. This was a different part of South Jersey, and it had a different atmosphere. We focused on saving our money and buying a property we could call our own. We wanted a home much bigger than the one we had owned. We enrolled our daughter in kindergarten at a school not far from where we were living. My wife decided to return to school to get additional training in the medical field. While I was working, she was in school. I was also in school in the evenings. We both wanted to get more education. The more education you have, the more money you can make.

I continued working at the factory, making the drive back and forth from our apartment to Pennsauken each day. Then, after several months, the company laid off me and some of my coworkers. I didn't crawl under a rock and cry "Woe is me." I bounced back up and told myself I had to keep going. I prayed to God faithfully, and he always provided for me, so I didn't worry too much about losing my job. I trusted in God, believing he would deliver me from this situation. In the week following my layoff, I went out job hunting and searched the newspapers for leads. I saw several ads seeking cabinet workers. I knew that was something I could do.

CHAPTER 17

I called up one of the companies and got an interview. The owner hired me on the spot. I said to myself, *God is good.* This small business made countertops and cabinets. When I started work, the foreman instructed me on how the shop made countertops. I was okay with that, but I wanted to show him an easier, quicker, and more cost-effective way to make backsplashes for the countertops. The foreman didn't appreciate my suggestions. I made some backsplashes my way, using less time and material. He didn't like them. I worked for that company for only a week or two. I had problem after problem with the foreman. I had experience working in cabinet shops. I knew how to make countertops, cabinets, and backsplashes. I thought I would share what I knew and show the company how to save money.

The owner came to me one day and said he had to let me go. I asked him why, and he said that he had to listen to his foreman but that he appreciated what I knew and wanted to share. I explained the problem I was having with the foreman and told the owner he could save money on material and time if we made backsplashes the way I suggested to the foreman. The owner agreed with me but said he could not go against his foreman. His foreman did not want me there. He told the owner to fire me, and the owner did. Once again I was the lone African American employee, and I suspected the foreman had an issue with my race.

I chalked it up as a bad experience, and I didn't give up. I hit the pavement once again, looking for another job. I prayed to God about my shortcomings. I continued to have faith in him, knowing he would always provide for me. I came across another cabinet shop that was hiring, and this one was only five minutes away from where I lived. I went to the shop and filled out an application. I talked to the foreman, and he was very impressed with my capability as a cabinetmaker and a carpenter. He hired me right away. The shop made kitchen cabinets and countertops, bathroom vanities, vanity tops, and special kitchen countertops for large homes that were being built in South Jersey. The company's products were in great demand, and the place stayed very busy. The foreman said employees worked only four days a week and were off on Friday. I thought it was spectacular to have a four-day workweek and to be paid well. After being hired, I went home and told my wife. I thanked God for the blessing.

I made new friends at the shop. I was working with nice people, and that included the foreman. Because I was taught cabinetmaking and carpentry in school and had worked in other cabinet shops, I felt right at home. My coworkers and I built countertops, cabinets, and other items to be installed in homes. I often volunteered to work on Friday, and since we were off on Friday, it was considered an overtime day. I wanted to make extra money so I could purchase a car. It was nice to have my mother-in-law's car at our disposal, but it wasn't like having our own. My wife and I planned to put aside all the money we could. We saved for a house and for a car. I thanked God for the job, the overtime, and my knowledge of the carpentry trade. I continued to go to class three nights a week to finish the course in architectural drafting. I hoped one day to become an architect, and I worked very hard to learn that trade. This was something I had up my sleeve, something I looked forward to mastering, but I left everything up to God.

As a veteran, I was blessed with the opportunity to use the GI Bill to go back to school. I thank God for that opportunity. I didn't want to waste any time, and I learned as much as I could. I always tell the young to go after all the knowledge they can obtain. My plan was to get everything I could get out of education, to learn as much as I could possibly learn, to master as much as I could possibly master, to be good at whatever I pursued, and to teach others. I try to encourage people, "You can become whatever you want, but it's all up to you. It's all about how badly you want it. Pray to God for spiritual wisdom, and have faith in God to deliver you from any obstacle you may face." One scripture verse that has stuck with me for a long time is Philippians 4:13, which says, "I can do all things through Christ which strengthens me." I tell people, "If you keep that in your heart, you can do all things, no matter what obstacle you face. God will give you the strength and the ability to do anything. All you have to do is ask, because God says, 'Ask and you shall receive; knock and the door shall be opened for you.'" I was taught these things as a young boy. I was taught by my mother. I was taught by the pastor of my church. These things have stayed with me as I have grown older, and I like to share them with other people.

My time working at the cabinet shop was wonderful. I was doing something I loved to do. I had good coworkers and a good foreman. The shop was close to home, so I could have lunch there and then return to work. God blessed me by allowing me to be that close to home. I made very good money, and I was well liked by my coworkers and by my foreman because I did my job exceedingly well.

One day the foremen lost his finger while cutting material on the table saw. The company was looking for someone to replace him since he would be out of work for some time. I was asked to take the job, but I wasn't sure when the foreman would return, so I declined the offer. He returned soon after. I thanked God for his quick recovery minus one finger. Everyone was glad to see him back at work. I continued making countertops and cabinets and installing them in homes. I did this for a year or two, but for some reason I wanted more.

My neighbor in the apartment above me worked for a small heating and air-conditioning company, and we became close. He was an ex-marine and I was ex-navy, and we joked with each other. One day he asked me if I would be interested in making a lot more money than I was making, and I said yes. He said he could get me hired at his company, but I said I had no skills in the plumbing and heating trade and didn't know if the company would want me. He told me not to worry, because the company had a big job and needed more men, so getting hired wouldn't be a problem. I thought about it and told him to let his boss know I was interested and to ask what would be required of me. After speaking to his boss, my neighbor told me his boss would hire me and wanted to know if I could start work on Monday. I was astonished to hear that. Though he didn't know me, the boss would hire me simply on my neighbor's word. I thought my neighbor must have a lot of clout at his company.

I told him I could not leave the cabinet shop without giving notice. The company had treated me very well, and I made good money. I was loyal to the people there, and they liked me and relied on my expertise. My neighbor passed this on to his boss, who agreed to give me at least two weeks before I started work. I wanted to give the cabinet shop two weeks' notice before I left. This way the company would have time to hire someone to replace me, and I could give the shop two more weeks of work before leaving. I thought this was the right thing to do.

The next day I told my foreman I was entering another line of work and gave him two weeks' notice. He was fine with that. He appreciated the fact that I thought enough of the shop to give two weeks' notice, because sometimes people just up and leave. I was taught to show courtesy to a company that hired you, because you might have to return there someday. If you leave on a bad note or without giving decent notice, you may not be able to return. So when you leave a job, give the company notice. One or two weeks' notice is acceptable.

CHAPTER 18

When I started work with my neighbor's company, he told me I didn't have to drive since we were going to the same place, and he invited me to ride with him. He introduced me to his boss, the foremen, and the workers, and they all welcomed me. I was grateful to be hired by this company. The owner wanted to hire veterans like me and my neighbor. I had no clue about air-conditioning and heating work, but I was willing to learn. The boss told me to go with my neighbor on service calls so I could get a feel for the work. My neighbor was very good with heating and air-conditioning systems, and he showed me what he knew. The work didn't seem too hard to learn. I have always been open to learning new things, so I paid careful attention as we went on jobs. I greatly appreciated the company hiring me, especially considering I was not a licensed electrician, plumber, or heating service guy. My job experience was in carpentry, cabinetmaking, and aircraft mechanics. I had always believed I could never learn too much.

As the days passed, I continued working with my neighbor, learning as much as I could about the trade. Then the company got a big service contract with an apartment complex up north. The work lasted for many months, and I found myself putting in very long hours. So did my neighbor and all the other workers on the job. We worked around the clock, trying to ensure that the people who lived in the complex would not be without water for any long period. We worked feverously every day, digging up the ground, fixing leaks, covering up pipes again, and getting boilers back on line with hot water in the apartment units. All of us were beat from working long hours seven days a week. Our wives rarely saw us because we were constantly on the job. The company was very grateful for our dedication and commitment and compensated us for the long hours and the cold nights we spent on this trying project in the dead of the winter.

The job finally was completed, with new piping and a whole new plumbing setup for the apartment complex. We were all assigned to different places for service repairs, and it was back to business as usual. I worked for the company for quite some time and was paid very well even though I wasn't an electrician or a plumber. I worked with my neighbor, who was a very good service mechanic, and we did many jobs without a problem. Our motto was to get the job done right the first time, and we did just that. My neighbor and I worked throughout New Jersey, and I learned a lot from him.

One day the company owner told me the firm was relocating to another part of South Jersey. He said he knew I had experience in carpentry and cabinetmaking and asked if I could draw up blueprints for the renovations to the new office and if I could do the renovations. I told the owner that I could but that he had to give me a couple of men to help with the renovations. He was pleased to hear that, and I was happy to be able to show him my expertise. The company gave me a truck so I could pick up supplies or go from job site to job site and help other mechanics with their work. I was pleased that the company trusted me enough to give me a vehicle. One day I met up with one of the managers. He took me to the new office and walked me through the place to get my insight on how to remodel it. As I toured the building, I thought about how I could convert it to office space. That evening when I got home, I made drawings of the building and of the areas where offices would be constructed. I included an office for each manager and for the owner of the company. I studied the drawings carefully and decided to present them to the owner the next day to see what his take would be. I was still attending the architectural drafting classes at night.

The things I had learned in those classes helped me a lot in making the drawings for the renovations, and I thanked God for his help. God has brought me through a lot, and I praise him and thank him for the knowledge he has given me to be able to achieve what I have achieved so far. I still have a long way to go, and I trust God will be there. As he said in his Word, "I will never leave you, nor forsake you," and I know that is true. God has been with me every step of the way. As I continue on my journey in life, I am eager to see what else he has in store for me and to achieve as much as I can achieve and to share it with others. I want other people to know that they can be whatever they want to be, that the sky is the limit. There is nothing stopping them from achieving whatever they want to achieve. My architectural classes got increasingly difficult, but I learned as much as I could. I knew one day that I would put it all together and that this skill would be very useful sometime in the future. That was one of the reasons I decided to go to school for architecture. I loved carpentry and cabinetmaking, and I began to love architecture. I knew that somehow, somewhere I would be able to apply it. Finally, after looking at the drawings I had made for the renovations, the owner decided to take me off of service calls and to use me exclusively on the office project. I made a list of the materials I needed for the renovations, and before long I was able to start doing them.

The owner gave me a coworker to help me get the project done. It took just three weeks to complete three offices in the building the company had acquired. The owner was very impressed with the speed of the renovations. He had also been impressed with the enclosures I designed and installed when the company was working at the huge apartment complex. I think he asked me to do these jobs because he was told about my carpentry experience. I enjoyed my job at the heating and air-conditioning company because I learned new things about these fields. Every day offered a different challenge. I never knew exactly what I would be doing from day to day. However, once we had finished the renovations to the building, I wondered where I would go from there. I wondered whether I would be returning to the field to work with the other service mechanics or whether the company would let me go. I didn't know, but I was very hopeful.

I returned to the field, but one day the owner of the company asked me if I would come over to his house to discuss some renovations he wanted done to his property. I was very excited and said yes. The next day when I arrived at work, the boss asked me to follow him to his house. When I got there, he took me into his kitchen and asked if I could give it an upgrade. I agreed to do the work and gave him my ideas for the renovation. After he had heard my plan, we agreed on how I would do the work. I thought this would be a quick and easy job. I ordered all the materials I needed, had them delivered to the house, and started the renovation. This was a major project, but I didn't have a problem with that. I rather enjoyed the opportunity to do a complete kitchen renovation and upgrade.

The boss told me to take all the time I needed to get the job done, and I explained to him that I would have the job done in a fairly short time. I worked alone at my own pace. It took me a week and a few days to complete the project. Each day the boss would check on my progress, and I could see from the look on his face that he was pleased with what he saw. When I completed the job, he and his wife were very happy with the outcome. He paid me well, and I appreciated the opportunity to do the work. I'm sure he passed the word to his neighbors and his friends and to all my coworkers. They heard about the renovations I did at the boss's home. I again thanked God for giving me the knowledge and the experience to do all the jobs I had done and for blessing me time after time. God has always been with me, and I thank him for that.

After completing the job at my boss's house, I returned to the field and worked with the other service mechanics on calls. I was glad to be back in the field. Then one day we had a service call at Mercer County airport in New Jersey. There was a heating and air-conditioning problem at the RCA aircraft hangar. I saw several aircraft in the hangar including a helicopter quite similar to one of the helicopters I used to work on when I was in the navy. I started to reminisce about my experiences as a jet mechanic in the navy working on helicopters. I briefly watched the mechanics working on the helicopter, and then my neighbor and I investigated the problem with the heating and air-conditioning system in the hangar. After several hours, we finally got the system working and headed home. On the way back, I talked about my feelings when I saw the helicopter, about the aircraft itself, about my experiences as a crew chief and a plane captain on helicopters, and about my flights in the military. I always love to share those experiences.

I continued my studies of architectural drafting. The classes were held several times a week. I learned more and more including architectural math and the standards for draftsmen. At this point I had about two years of schooling. The school would get calls from companies looking for junior draftsmen, and I was among several students given the opportunity to visit one company to be interviewed and to take an oral exam to see if we could get hired. I was the only African American in my class selected to be interviewed for a job as a junior draftsman. I was excited about this opportunity and told my wife about my selection. With my experience as a draftsman, I thought I had a good chance of getting a job. I had to take off from my job to visit the company.

The interview went well. I then went through the oral exam. The company made prefab concrete parts and concrete structures. I thought it would be a good place to work as a junior draftsman after completing school. I knew I didn't have too far to go before finishing the course, and I was happy to be given the opportunity to apply for a job like this. I prayed about it and left everything up to God. The other candidates and I were asked to sit in the waiting room while company personnel made their decision on a junior draftsman. Finally the interviewer began calling us in one at a time. When my turn came, I entered the office and the interviewer told me, "Sorry, but we will not be hiring any junior draftsmen at this time." When I spoke to my classmates, they all said they were told the same thing.

All of us were disappointed at the outcome, but I knew the reason and let it go at that. I returned home and shared what happened with my wife and my neighbor. I explained that the interview had gone well but that the company didn't hire anyone sent from the school. I continued to attend classes a few days a week, but I started to have reservations about where I was going with architectural drafting. I wondered if it was a good or a bad idea to become a draftsman. I needed to land a good permanent job, one that would offer me security. I had a family and I knew my wife would be expecting another child in the near future. I had been through quite a few jobs, and now I wanted something stable, a job I could retire from in twenty or thirty years. I loved working for the heating and air-conditioning company, but I knew deep down inside that this was not a job I wanted to have for twenty or thirty years.

I thought about getting a job at RCA working as a mechanic on the company's aircraft. I also thought about a job at the Philadelphia Naval Shipyard that someone had brought to my attention. That would be another job from which I could retire after a certain number of years. So I considered both places—RCA and the Philadelphia Naval Shipyard. One day I decided to put in an application at the shipyard. Several older people had advised me to get a job that offered security. They recommended that I look for a job at the Philadelphia Naval Shipyard because that would be a government job. I would have job security working for the government plus my military time would be added, and I could retire at an early age. I gave it a lot of thought and applied for a job at the shipyard, hoping for the best.

I continued to work at the heating and air-conditioning company, and after a month I forgot about the job at the shipyard. My wife and I saved our money, hoping one day to leave the apartment and to buy a house. We wanted a place we could call our own. We often talked about how so many people lived in apartments year after year and in the end owned nothing. My wife and I decided early in our marriage that we would focus on obtaining property that we could own in thirty years. That was our goal. I had plenty of work at the heating and air-conditioning company. I got along with my coworkers, I got raises, and I got comfortable. Then one day I received a letter from the Philadelphia Naval Shipyard saying I had been accepted for the shipwright apprenticeship program. I was overjoyed and excited, and I thanked God for blessing me again. I thought about how my boss would handle the news that I would be leaving the company and moving on to bigger and better things. I finally approached him the week after I got the letter and said I had been accepted at the shipyard and would be leaving for my new place of employment.

My boss was happy for me and said the company appreciated my work as a service mechanic and as a carpenter. He thanked me for helping the company and for renovating his kitchen. The owner also said that if some reason I ever wanted to come back, he would always have an opening for me. I felt very good about that because this wasn't the first company to have made me such an offer. I have received these offers because of the respect I have for people, the professionalism of my work, my ability to get along with others, and my general demeanor. My boss made me feel very special, and his kind words showed once again that when you do good to other people, it comes back to you. Fortunately, I wouldn't have to start at the shipyard for a month, so I had plenty of time to gather my things and to get ready. I gave my boss two weeks' notice, which he appreciated, and continued to do my job. When my final day at the company arrived, I said my goodbyes and everyone wished me well.

Shortly after I left the company, I quit the architectural drafting course. I was concerned about the pressure on my eyes caused by continually reading small print, and I was disappointed that I had been turned down when I applied for a job. I still wanted to become an architect, so I gave a lot of thought to my decision. However, I knew that even though I quit the school, I still had that experience under my belt. I knew if I decided to return to school, or if I wanted to do some drawings for someone, I still had the knowledge and the experience to do that. My architectural studies were something else I could mark off as accomplished along with so many other things I had done in my life. I decided to move on and to get ready to start my job as a shipwright apprentice at the Philadelphia Naval Shipyard.

My wife and I desperately wanted to buy a house. We had plenty of money saved up and were constantly looking for a nice place. I had quit my job and had two weeks left before starting my new one, so we were looking for a house in South Jersey. We finally came out to the Sicklerville area. We'd seen a real estate agent there who had showed us several homes in the area, and we loved what we saw. But we especially loved one house after looking at all the others. We wanted to make it the house of our dreams.

We spoke with the real estate agent, filled out the paperwork, and contacted a mortgage company. Then we awaited word on our application. Meanwhile, we were still anxiously waiting to hear from the real estate agent. We happened to come along at the right time, and our bid on the house was successful. Then we were approved for the mortgage. It was amazing how God worked things out. I had been through a lot of jobs after leaving the military. But I had been blessed to get good jobs and to be able to maintain my family, to save money, and to buy our dream house. God blessed me with all of it. Finally, we had the closing on the house just before my start date at the Philadelphia Naval Shipyard. A lot of things had been happening in my life, and now my wife was pregnant with our second child. With so many blessings bestowed upon me, I was happy and was grateful to God. At last we moved into the house. We are still in that house today. I was beat from the moving process, and I was starting work at the shipyard in a couple of days.

CHAPTER 19

After arriving to begin work at the Philadelphia Naval Shipyard, I filled out all the required paperwork, attended the welcome sessions, and learned when I would start classes. I was assigned to shop 64, set aside for shipwrights. A shipwright is a ship's carpenter. I believe I was hired as a shipwright apprentice mainly because of my skills as a carpenter and a cabinetmaker. I would work on ships three days a week and would attend shipwright school for two days. After four years of apprenticeship training and of work in the field, and after passing all the exams, I would be a shipwright journeyman.

All of this was new to me. I had never worked on a ship or a dry dock before. I didn't know what a dry dock was. There was a lot I needed to learn about the job of a shipwright, and as always I was eager to learn. Safety was the most important lesson I had to learn—safety in the dry dock, safety working aboard ships. I had to learn about working on a ship and about the classifications and the types of ships. I also had to learn how to operate equipment in the sawmill, the area where we would manufacture bilge blocks and keel blocks for the ships. Those blocks would go to the dry dock for docking and undocking the ships. I had so much to learn, but this was a good experience for me, something completely different from all the jobs I'd had in the past. I was open to learning as much as I could about the shipwright trade. I thanked God for my new job. I believed it was the one I had been looking for.

I had an excellent instructor in the apprenticeship program, one of the best in the shipwright trade. He taught me everything I needed to know about the trade. I spent two days in a classroom and three days working on the ships. All of that had to come together in order for me to be a successful shipwright. I looked forward to becoming a journeyman one day, and four years seemed like a long time to get to that point, but again, there was a lot to learn. But yes, you could learn everything about the shipwright trade in four years. Actually you could learn it in less than four years depending on the instruction you received and on the experience you got on board the ships, working in a dry dock, in the sawmill, or with the other shipboard tradesmen. You could also learn a lot from the sailors on the ships.

The good times, the people I met, the knowledge I gained—this was an experience I would cherish. The shipwright trade is one of the best trades because the shipwright has many duties. Some of the other trades have only limited functions. The shipwright is responsible for so much—docking and undocking the ships, laying out bilge blocks and keel blocks in the dry dock, and making these blocks in the sawmill. The shipwright is also responsible for the ships' flooring, the berthing spaces, the rubber matting, the electronic spaces, the combat information center, and the bridge. The shipwright must also erect scaffolding on the ship and in the dry dock so the other trades so can do their jobs safely.

The shipwright is also responsible for setting up instruments inside a ship's fuel and water tanks so their contents can be monitored on the bridge and in the pilot house. All the other trades look to the shipwrights to establish reference points for installing platforms on ships. The shipwright must also lay out the waterlines on a ship so the painters can paint them. The shipwright also establishes a ship's draft lines. In four years of training, you must learn all of a shipwright's duties. What you don't learn in the classroom, you learn on the job— on the ship, in the dry dock, in the sawmill. All of these things come together, and you store them in your mind forever. That's why I think the shipwright trade is one of the best trades in the shipyard. I was happy to be a part of that trade.

After my indoctrination, I reported to shop 64. I was introduced to the foreman and to all the men in the shop. The shipyard had five dry docks, and shop 64 also extended out to dry docks four and five. However, as an apprentice, I started in dry dock three. Once I arrived in the shop, I was given a list of tools that I would need to get for myself. Other tools could be obtained from the tool crib. A couple of shipwright journeymen walked me through the dry dock area and a hundred steps down into the dry dock. They explained the purpose of a dry dock, of keel blocks, of bilge blocks, of concrete blocks, and of the caisson. The caisson was an area that separated the dry dock from the river—in this case, the Delaware River. We then visited the sawmill where shipwrights manufactured blocks made of oak. These blocks would be cut a certain way and would be set up in a dry dock as cradle blocks on which a ship would land once it was docked. Those big timbers were an interesting sight.

The sawmill also housed a huge tank used to make wood water resistant. A special treatment was added to the water, and the wood remained in the tank for a certain number of days. The green wood looked like the pressure-treated wood we buy today, and the shipyard used a similar process to produce wood. The wood used for bilge blocks and keel blocks had to be treated because those blocks were in constant use and were often underwater. A ship entering a dry dock was sitting in the water for a long time before the water was drained from the dry dock. The blocks had to be specially treated so they would last a long time. This was another function of a shipwright. We next boarded a ship in the dry dock. This was the first time I had ever been aboard a ship. I wondered what kind of work we did on these ships, and the journeymen told me to remember what I was taught, to remember the parts and the functions of a ship and how to set up the dry dock for the docking and the undocking of ships. I knew this was an important point because one day I would be responsible for this. We went farther inside the ship, and that was the lesson for the day.

The next day I got a chance to work with some of the other shipwright journeymen erecting scaffolding. They showed me the correct procedure for building pipe scaffolding. This was not like regular scaffolding that can be bought or rented. This was two-and-a-half-inch and three-inch pipe along with the fittings used to connect the pipes. A shipwright had to know all this and a lot more. The journeymen were giving me a little bit of schooling. My shop foremen had the men show me the responsibilities of the shipwright trade. In one part of our shop was the boat crew. These guys were responsible for building and maintaining the captain's jig, which was made from fiberglass. The captain's jig is a smaller boat that the captain uses when leaving the ship and it was just for the captain. Members of the boat crew were called boat builders, and they were part of the shipwright trade. There was so much to learn, and I looked forward to my first day in apprenticeship class.

The class started the following week, and we were told about the materials and the books we would need. The instructor gave us the books we would work out of, and these books contained information and instruction on the shipwright trade. We started off with the job description and the classification of a shipwright and learned a shipwright's duties. Then we learned about the tools a shipwright uses when he's erecting scaffolding, working in the sawmill, setting up the dry dock, and docking or undocking a ship.

We were taught the functions of a navigational transit and how to use one. We were also taught how make and to use water bottles. A water bottle is a water level, and we would use these water bottles to determine how much a ship might be listing to port or to starboard as it sat in the dry dock. We would stretch the water bottles from port to starboard and would use them to get a reading. We also learned how to lay out an area for floor tile or rubber matting. We were also instructed on how to prepare the floors, because all ship decks are made of steel. And we had to prepare the floors with an underlayment almost like a cement mix. We would down put the underlayment, and then we would lay out the floor and strike our lines, marking off everything so we had a starting point for laying our tile. We were instructed on the math we needed to make calculations when we had to do regulating. Regulating was done to establish reference lines on the ship, and we had to know how to establish those lines. It was important that we did this correctly because we would give these reference lines to the other trades so they could erect platforms on the ship. The other trades would always look to the shipwright to supply them with the information they needed.

A shipwright's job could be very dangerous. We were out in the heat of the summer and the cold of the winter. We were down in the dry docks in every season, doing whatever was needed to dock or to undock a ship, setting up or disassembling the blocks. The decks were very hot in the summer and very cold in the winter. They were freezing in the winter because they were made of steel. We had to make sure we wore gloves because our bare hands would stick to the steel. A ship in a dry dock or a long pier is a very cold place in the winter, especially when the wind is blowing off of the Delaware River. This was a job not too many people could do. I saw guys drop out of the apprenticeship program because they could not survive it. The worst problem was working outdoors in the heat and the cold.

We built scaffolding more than a hundred feet off of the deck of a ship. We wore our safety belts and always watched each other's backs. This was very important because a shipyard is a dangerous place to work. I recognized that when I was in dry dock three, working on smaller ships, light destroyers, and helicopter carriers, but dry dock five was made for aircraft carriers, and working on an aircraft carrier is extremely dangerous. That's true not only in a shipyard but at sea on the flight deck. So I knew I had to watch out for myself and for my partner and always put safety first. On board a ship, I was always conscious about where I was walking and made sure I knew the ship from the upper to the lower decks. All of this was taught in the apprenticeship class, but we learned how to get from one point to another just by being on the ships. That's hard on some of the small ships, but it's three or four times harder on an aircraft carrier, which is so much bigger than ships such as destroyers and light destroyers.

I progressed in my apprenticeship studies, and I found the tests we took very simple. We were tested every week on the information we got in class and on the information we acquired while working out in the field. This included what we experienced on board ships, down in the dry docks, or in the sawmill. We were tested on a lot of this stuff in class, and I always did very well. Time flew by, and I was now in the third year of the apprenticeship program. I was given jobs to perform and worked alongside several journeymen. I had my first big job in that third year, working with a couple of journeymen on an admiral's flagship. I learned a lot working on that ship, including information about the ship itself, such as where its apartments were located. I found the job very interesting. My foreman had me work along with one of the journeymen, and the two of us were responsible for installing rubber matting on the deck in some of the ship's electronic spaces. When we were done with that, we installed new floor tile in other areas, including the berthing spaces. We also did scaffolding work. It was the first time I'd been on a ship that big.

The apprenticeship program was nearing an end, and I wondered if I would pass the final exam. I always did well on tests, but I felt uneasy because our instructor had set strict requirements for this exam. I wanted to study hard so I could remember everything I was taught in the classroom and on the ships. I was very fortunate because the guy I worked with on the ships and in the sawmill remembered my instructor from his own classroom days several years earlier. My partner told me what to expect on the exam but said I should simply remember what he and the other mechanics had taught me out in the field and not worry about the test. That made me feel very good. My partner and my foreman had a lot of confidence in me, and many other people I worked with knew the type of mechanic I was and saw how much I had learned about the shipwright trade. So I had a lot of people supporting me. They were happy to see I had reached the end of my four-year apprenticeship and was ready to take the final exam.

Once I had passed the exam and had completed the course, I would be a journeyman shipwright. The support I got from my shop foreman and from all of my workmates gave me more confidence in myself. As the exam neared, I prayed about it to God, asking him to instruct me and to give me the ability to remember what I had been taught so I could do well. I knew that God had always been with me and was responsible for every job I'd had and every promotion I'd gotten. He wouldn't let me down. I knew I would pass that exam with flying colors. I studied every night after I got home from work at the shipyard. I had my wife ask me questions that I thought might appear on the exam. As I studied, I thought about everything God had brought me through—from my childhood days in the inner city of Philadelphia, to my time in the navy, to the years after I had left the military. Since exiting the navy, I had never been without a job for long. I thanked God for doing so much.

The day had finally come. I studied the night before, got a good night's sleep, and I was well prepared for the test. I drove to the shipyard, entered the classroom, and sat down with my classmates. I wasn't nervous that morning. I was confident I would do very well on the test. The instructor handed out the test and told us the amount of time we had to complete it. Once we were done, we were to report to our work areas in the shipyard. We would be notified of the test results within a week if not sooner. After completing the exam, I headed for the ship where I was assigned to work. My work partner asked me how I thought I had done on the test, and I told him I thought I had done very well. I thought the test was easier than everybody had said it would be, so I was confident I had gotten a good score. Now all I had to do was wait for the results and move forward from there. I had started working at the shipyard in 1978, and it seemed like only yesterday. Four years had gone by, and I had completed the apprentice program for shipwright. It had been a quick four years, and I had learned a lot about the shipwright trade. I felt very fortunate to have been selected to work at the Philadelphia Naval Shipyard.

Several days went by, and finally the results arrived. I had passed the test with flying colors and was now a journeyman shipwright. I was very happy, and so were all of my workmates. My best buddy, my partner in the shipyard, was pleased to learn I had done well on the test. He was happy to be able to work with me as a fellow journeyman. I was very honored to be a journeyman, and I knew God had brought me through another challenge in life. I could add this to my list of accomplishments. None of them had been easy, but I was determined to attain whatever goal I pursued. I always remembered a Bible verse I have held dear, Philippians 4:13, which says, "I can do all things through Christ which strengthens me."

Now that I was a journeyman shipwright, my foreman made me lead mechanic on several new jobs on the ships. He trusted me enough to give me that position. I continued working with the shipyard partner who had worked alongside me while I was in apprentice training. He would check to see how I was doing on the new jobs. I was responsible for gathering the material needed to erect pipe scaffolding on board the ship and in the dry dock if necessary. I was also to assist in laying out the dry dock for a ship, and that entailed making differently shaped blocks in the sawmill for the bilge and for the keel. My work in the dry dock and my training in school paid off because I knew exactly how to proceed with laying out the dry dock. I also knew how to set up the dry dock for ships when they returned to the shipyard for overhauls.

I was confident about everything I was doing in the shipyard and felt fortunate that my boss had given me the opportunity to lead several jobs. All of the other mechanics who worked with me followed my lead, and the jobs turned out very well.

During my time in the shipyard, I worked on quite a few ships, including helicopter carriers, destroyers, light destroyers, flagships, and aircraft carriers. I can't remember all of their names, but I spent a lot of time working on each one of those ships. I helped lay out the dry dock for the ships before they came in, and I was responsible for docking and undocking them. I also helped build scaffolding on board ships and in the dry dock. I assisted with regulating on the ships, establishing reference points for the other trades, which were responsible for manufacturing structures and installing them on the ships. I also helped establish reference points for the safe parking lines to be painted on the flight decks of aircraft and helicopter carriers.

A shipwright is responsible for many things. It's a very challenging job, but carpentry skills make it much easier. A shipyard is not an easy place to work. The dry docks and the ships are very dangerous places, and not many people last. Some people get jobs at the shipyard and are surprised at how hard the work can be. That's true no matter what trade they're in. There's no easy job at the shipyard. Not everyone can do that kind of work. The weather is also a major factor. The winter is very cold in the dry dock, and the summer heat also makes the work extra hard. Docking and undocking a ship are among the toughest jobs at the shipyard. You're outside in the elements. If you're sighting a ship as it's coming into the dry dock, you'll be standing at the head of the dock, looking in the transit, taking your gloves off so you can adjust it, and putting them back on. You may be working high in the sky on the mast of a ship, building scaffolding out of a bucket on a crane. You're on and off of a platform while doing this. Sometimes you'll have to step onto the scaffold and latch on to something with your safety belt to ensure you won't fall. Winter and summer make all this work much harder.

Though the shipyard was very dangerous, I loved my job because it was a challenge. I think everyone who spent year after year at the shipyard got accustomed to the work and to the temperatures in the summer and the winter. I got used to it. In fact, I enjoyed every minute of every day I worked at the shipyard, every ship I worked on, every dry dock I laid out, every ship I sighted in as it entered the dry dock. I loved every bit of it. I thank God for that. I also know my mother prayed for me and for the rest of my siblings, asking God to protect us in everything we did. I think because she prayed and because God watched over me, I survived a dangerous job. I worked in the dry dock, on board the ships, high on the masts of the ships, and in the tanks of the ships. (Some people were claustrophobic and couldn't work there.)

A special class of people worked in the shipyard, and I enjoyed my job as a shipwright. We worked in all types of weather. When it rained, we worked. If it snowed, we worked. There was no timeout because each ship that came to the shipyard for an overhaul faced a deadline for completion of the work. We worked every day without fail to finish by the completion date, if not sooner. Sometimes I was sent with other shipyard workers to another state to evaluate a ship and to decide what the ship would need when it came to Philly for an overhaul. That was a part of the shipwright's job that I learned in the apprenticeship program. This inventory had to be done years before the ship was due to come to the shipyard. Other trades also had a part in planning and estimating. I was selected on several occasions to be part of a planning and estimating team for my shop. This was because my foreman had seen how effective I was as a shipwright, how seriously I took my job, and how well I did my work. That was another of my accomplishments, and I thank God for it.

My job as a shipwright was challenging from time to time. Sometimes I would do an inlay in a floor tile, and the ship's quartermaster would ask for something different in the tile, perhaps an insignia. I could do whatever officers wanted done as long as it was a part of the schedule on board the ship. If there was tile to be done, I did it and sometimes I would add something extra to the design. This was exciting for me because I love to work with floor tile. I also worked in the sawmill, making blocks and doing special projects for the ships and doing other work for the shipyard.

In shop 64 we were responsible for much of the overhaul work on ships. In 1983 we did a lot of work on a navy ship with a special completion deadline. I was a part of the overhaul team, and we were given letters of commendation from the commander of the Philadelphia

Naval Shipyard and from the shipyard's production officer for a job well done. That was very special for me and for the people who worked with me on the overhaul. I had worked on many ships, but this was the only time I had received letters of commendation from the shipyard commander and production officer.

My five years at the shipyard had been very good with no layoffs and constant work. I had finished my four-year apprenticeship training and was now a journeyman. I enjoyed my job, and God had been good to me. In 1983 he blessed me and my wife with another child, Thomas Jr. We now had three children—two girls and a boy. I was constantly busy in the carpentry trade. Whenever someone needed a home repair or renovation, I was available. I hardly ever turned down work. I guess I was a workaholic. Even though I worked at the shipyard and made pretty good money, I wanted to give my family the best, so I always jumped at the chance to do work on the outside. I spent time after working hours at the shipyard and on weekends, preferably Saturdays. I'd usually save Sunday for church. While installing floor tiles on a ship, I was approached by a much older man who worked in another trade at the shipyard. He asked me if I did tile like that on the outside. "What type of work are you looking to have done?" I asked. He said he wanted to have his bathroom retiled, and I told him I would be more than happy to come over and look at the job to see if I could do it for him. I decided to do the bathroom renovation and other work at his house in the weeks following.

One morning at the shipyard, I was not feeling well, but I carried on and went aboard a ship to start the job I was supposed to do. I had a couple of new guys working with me to disassemble pipe scaffolding way above the main deck, and I wasn't comfortable with them. I was used to working with people who had experience disassembling pipe scaffolding, especially when it was up high on the ship. We knew how to work with each other. When you work with people for a long time, you begin to know their work habits, and they know yours. On this day a new guy was told to work along with me and the other guys. I hadn't had the chance to work with him, so I didn't know much about how he operated.

We were more than a hundred feet above the main deck when we started to disassemble the pipes scaffolding. And as we were removing the pipe scaffolding, we were taking the scaffold planks and putting them on a platform held by the crane. The new guy grabbed the scaffold plank and handed it to me so I could put it onto the cart. The plank was twenty feet long, and I was straddling the pipe scaffolding. When he gave me the plank, he let his end go and I wasn't ready. I didn't think he was going to let his end go, and I slipped because of the weight and the length of the plank. I let the plank fall, and then I fell fifteen or twenty feet. For a moment I felt like I was floating in space. Then I felt like I had been lifted up by someone or something after my hand went through a bolt attached to a turnbuckle that supported the cables on the mast. The turnbuckle saved me. My hand landed directly on it, and the rod on the turnbuckle went through my hand, and that's what saved me. I was hurt but safe and alive.

I thought for a moment that I was going to die, but God was watching over me and saved me. I believe God sent his angels to catch me when I fell, because there was nothing else there besides that turnbuckle. I'd done pipe scaffolding installation and disassembling plenty of times on plenty of masts way up high and had never experienced anything like this before. I think this accident happened because the new guy wasn't familiar with the way we worked and assumed I had full control of the scaffold plank when he handed it over to me. When you're working high above a ship, you have to be careful and to understand the guys you're working with. If not, somebody's going to get hurt or killed.

I was fortunate. This accident could have been worse. Usually when I'm up high, I tie my safety harness to some part of the scaffolding, but that day for some reason I forgot to do that. Thank God I was saved from that fall. I went to the infirmary, got a tetanus shot, had my hand bandaged, and was sent back to work. When I returned to the ship I wanted to speak to the new guy to explain to him the importance of safety, but he had also gone to the infirmary. Someone told me to go back to the shop and to take it easy for the rest of the day, and that was fine with me. I was shaken up by what had happened and I needed that break. As I finished the day in the shop, I thought about how blessed I was to have been saved from death or serious injury, and I thanked

God for watching over me. I went home that evening and tried to forget about what had happened that day.

The weekends go by pretty quickly when you're busy. Suddenly, Monday would arrive, and I would be back at the shipyard, back to the place where I loved to work. Every day was different; every day offered a new challenge. The shipwright trade offers so many things to do, and that's what I loved about my job at the Philadelphia Naval Shipyard. Sometimes I would work on a different ship every day, sometimes I would spend a month on one ship, and sometimes I would work on one ship the whole time it was in Philly for its overhaul. As a journeyman shipwright, I could work in any shipyard whether it was a government shipyard or a private shipyard. I loved that idea. If you have a trade, you can go anywhere with it. I can work anywhere as a carpenter. I can take my skills as a draftsman anywhere. I can read blueprints wherever I want. My work as a jet mechanic in the navy gives me the opportunity to work at any airport I choose; I can go anywhere I want in the aviation field. God gave me the wisdom and the ability to learn all these things, and I'm thankful for that. I want to use every bit of knowledge I have been given and perhaps help someone else out.

One day my shop foreman confirmed the talk I'd heard that the shipyard was seeking applications for two foremen at shop 64. The shipyard wanted a new foreman for my shop and an additional foreman because the shop had more people and plenty of work from dry dock two to dry dock five. Several people, including my foreman and some of my coworkers, encouraged me to apply for the position. I had been working as a journeyman shipwright for several years and knew the trade very well. I knew what was necessary to work as a shop foreman. As a people person, I knew how to deal with others. I knew how to talk to them. So I considered applying for the position. Many people told me I had a good chance of being appointed because of my experience as a journeyman shipwright and because of my ability to get jobs done. They said that they wanted someone with knowledge and time spent in the shipyard and that I would be the perfect candidate. I would also be the only African American who was qualified to apply for the position. I finally decided to do it.

I had no idea what the application for the position would require or what type of questioning I would face in the oral exam. But I thought I could handle whatever they threw at me. I continued doing my daily tasks at the shipyard and prepared myself for the exam for shop foreman. I also continued to do outside work. I got lots of offers because people knew the professionalism of my work. I also enjoyed remodeling; it was one of my trades. I enjoyed working in a shipyard. This was a gift God had given me, and I loved the job. But I couldn't let my work at the shipyard and the side jobs become too much of a distraction. I had to stay focused on the exam I was going to take. I reviewed everything I was taught in the apprenticeship program and everything I learned after I became a journeyman. I looked at my work experience, at my responsibilities as a shipwright, and at the responsibilities of a foreman. This was a lot to consider and I felt a bit overwhelmed. I was excited about the possibility of becoming shipwright foreman. I knew that would look good on my résumé if I decided to leave the shipyard. A lot of people were backing me because they were confident I would make a good foreman for shop 64. I prayed about this, asking God to point me in the right direction, to give me the wisdom to do well on the test, to handle the oral exam, and to fulfill my responsibilities as a shipwright foreman if I got the job.

I had a lot on my plate, but I was looking forward to becoming foreman. I heard the word was out around the shipyard that I was going to take the test for shop foreman. And many guys in my shop said they were happy to learn I was going to take the exam. And I was very happy to hear that all these guys thought I would easily pass the test and be selected as shop foreman. I felt pretty good about that, but I soon got a surprise. One of the heads of shop 64 was going to allow a relative to apply for the position. At that point the other two candidates and I didn't worry too much about this. The new challenger did not have the years of experience or the training to be considered for the position. The three of us weren't happy with the shop head's decision, but we could do nothing about it. We thought about protesting, but we decided it wasn't worth the effort.

The three other candidates and I took the written exam, and then we were called in one at a time for the oral exam by the shop head and a few other senior shop foremen. After the oral exam they asked us to return to our work areas and said they would get in touch with us as soon as they made their decision. I thought I did very well on the written and oral exams. Several weeks went by, and I said to myself, *This must be a very hard decision for them to make.* Finally we were all called in to hear the decision of the shop heads. And to my amazement and everyone else's the person selected as foreman was the relative of the head of the shop. He chose his relative to be foreman even though this guy had little experience and had been at the shipyard for only a year if that much. How could he be selected as shop foreman? I was very disappointed as were many others in shop 64. I decided to file a grievance over the shop head's choose his relative as foreman.

The process was very short. I lost the case. It was his word against mine, so I decided to let it go and to let God handle things for me. I realized it was probably God's purpose for me not to get the job as foreman. I thought God might have another purpose for me somewhere else some other time. A week or two later, my shop foreman told me the shop head, the person I had filed a grievance against, wanted me transferred to the dry dock four and five area where he was in charge. I knew this guy would make life difficult for me once I got to that area and was working under him. I prayed about the situation every day and I said, "God, just watch over me as I work in the shipyard, and let no harm come to me in any form or fashion." Before long I was transferred to that end of the shipyard. This area was a big change from dry docks two and three where I had worked before. The men worked on bigger ships, mostly aircraft carriers. It was a completely different world for me, but I adjusted to it. I continued doing outside jobs on weekends and loved what I was doing.

I stayed in that area of the shipyard and worked under that shop head for some time. As the months passed, he made life very difficult for me. He would reprimand me for bogus reasons. I believe he was trying to get even with me for filing a grievance against him for hiring his relative as shop 64 foreman. Despite all the reprimands, I decided to continue to do my work as a shipwright. I enjoyed working on the aircraft carriers and the helicopter carriers. Working on the big ships was a brand-new experience for me. I also had the opportunity to work with the men docking the aircraft carriers. This was a difficult operation. Looking at the size of the dry dock, I would think, *How could an aircraft carrier fit into this dry dock?* Appearances can be deceiving, but docking a carrier in that dry dock was a close call because we had a building very close to the dry dock. However, the docking operation was calculated down to the inches. Still, once the aircraft carrier was in the dry dock the edge of the flight deck was only a few feet from the building.

Every day I worked in the shipyard, I knew I would face a different challenge. I looked forward to those challenges and was confident I could meet them, no matter what. I continued to go to work and to do my job, and after working in the shipyard I would come home, relax, and spend time with my family.

I remembered how my father had told me I was spending too much time away from home and away from my family. He said I needed to spend more time with my wife and kids. I realized he was right and I took his advice. I was glad to have had that talk with my dad and to have made that change. I decided to spend more time at home with my wife and my three children. The change felt good. My weekends were free for me, my wife, and my children. It had been quite a while since I'd had this quality time with my family. After speaking to my father, I remembered the way I was raised. The eight of us children had a mother and a father at home, and we learned good family values from them. My father had a talk with me to refresh my memory about the way I was raised. People don't always get the chance to have a mother and father at home to learn family values. There are a lot of single-parent families—most of the time just a mother and no father—and it's hard for kids to grow up with good values when they don't have both parents to instill those values in them. I appreciate what was instilled in me and in my other brothers and sisters growing up. We were given good family values from my mother and my father. I had to remember how I was raised. I wanted my kids to be raised the same way and maybe better. I wanted to provide much more for them than I had when I was being raised. I needed to hear what my father told me.

Occasionally I would be offered overtime work on Saturdays. I would take it but not all of the time. I wanted to spend time with my family, but Saturday overtime was different from weekday overtime because once I was done I would be right back home. I wasn't away from home too much, not as much as I was in the past. I would usually accept overtime because there wasn't too much being offered. I noticed we were not getting many ships in for overhauls. I remembered the rumors I had heard about the shipyard closing in the near future. I gave this some thought because I always liked to be prepared. That was something I was taught in the military and as a Boy Scout. I wanted to be ahead of the game, and I began considering another job. I wanted something I knew would be secure since I didn't know how long the shipyard would be open. I had overheard workers talking about the shipyard closing, but I had also heard these guys talking about companies that were hiring. One of the companies was Boeing Helicopter in Ridley Park, Pennsylvania. Most of the guys who were talking had no experience in the aeronautical industry. However, I thought about my experience as a navy jet mechanic. I thought it would be a good idea to apply for a position as a jet mechanic to see what openings Boeing Helicopter might have.

I gave it some thought and decided to use my leave time to take a ride to Boeing Helicopter in Ridley Park. I didn't know where that was, but I'd heard conversations about where it was located. I decided to rely on that information and to drive up to Boeing Helicopter. I'd had several jobs since I got out of the navy. I thought a government-funded job at the navy shipyard would be there until I was ready to retire, but nothing is permanent. I wanted to stay ahead of the game. If the shipyard closed, I didn't want to be left out in the cold, trying to find a job. I decided to put in an application at Boeing Helicopter.

A few weeks after making this decision, I took time off, drove to Boeing Helicopter in Ridley Park, and filled out an application, citing my experience as an aviation jet mechanic in the navy. I did not specify the type of job I was applying for at Boeing. I thought the company would decide where to place me if it hired me. After filling out the application, I went home and prayed to God, saying I would be thankful for a good position at Boeing. I thanked him for all he had blessed me with and for keeping me safe in the past. I thought the shipyard would never close because there was always work. Ships were always coming in for overhauls. I remembered working on a ship and seeing it return years later for another overhaul. I was reminded of how long I had worked at the shipyard and of how many kinds of jobs I had done on different types and classes of ships. I thanked God for the opportunity to work in such a place and to learn the things I had learned. I had a long résumé based on my work at the shipyard. I knew I could get a job at any shipyard, government or private, mainly because of my experience and my title, journeyman shipwright. That was something I had under my belt, and I thanked God for that.

I thought I would be hired at Boeing. God is an awesome God, and he's a provider. God has brought me through so much, and I'm very grateful to him.

I continued working at the shipyard, waiting for it to close. That seemed like a real possibility. Ships weren't coming in the way they had been years before. When I started at the shipyard in 1978, all classes of ships were constantly arriving for overhauls. As time went by the number of ships coming in for overhauls decreased. That was a sign that the closure of the Philadelphia Naval Shipyard was coming. The shipyard had operated since the nineteenth century and had its heyday during the Second World War. If you take the Interstate 95 bridge heading to the airport, you can look to the left and see the old ships in mothballs still sitting in a back channel of the Philadelphia Naval Shipyard. A mothballed ship is one preserved and put away for possible future use. People put away clothes for the season, storing them in bags with mothballs to preserve them for future years. The compartments of those ships were sealed, ready to be opened any time the ships were needed again. And that was the most beautiful thing about the Philadelphia Naval Shipyard. I'm sure there are other shipyards in the country where ships have been mothballed. The ships are sitting there, well preserved, waiting for the opportunity to return to action.

Several weeks after applying for a job at Boeing Helicopter, I told my work partner what I had done. This guy was ten years my senior, and he and I were close. We understood each other; we had worked together for many years until I got transferred to the other part of the shipyard. However, I got a chance to work with many other shipwrights at that end of the shipyard, and I became pretty close to all these mechanics. I also told those guys I had applied for a job at Boeing, and they were all surprised to hear that. All of them said they would hate to see me leave.

These guys had worked with me for quite a while, and we got used to each other. We knew each other's work habits, and that's why I believe they expressed concern about me leaving. But I believed God had put me in the shipyard only for a season, to experience something, to learn something, and then to move on. And I believed that to the point where I was confident I would get a job at Boeing, though I didn't know what type of job that would be.

I was quite sure God would bless me with a job at Boeing based on my experience as a navy jet mechanic and my faith in him, and lo and behold, just a few weeks after I put in my application, I got home from work and there was a letter from Boeing Helicopter. I was busy working in the shipyard, and I had forgotten about the application. Now that I had the letter in my hand, I was quite hesitant about opening it. I wasn't sure my application had been accepted. I finally opened up the letter and read it. I had indeed been accepted at Boeing Helicopter. The company had reviewed my application and wanted me to come in to take a physical and to do paperwork that was required before I started work. I was full of joy when I got the letter, and I could not believe my good fortune.

CHAPTER 20

I showed my wife the letter saying I was hired at Boeing Helicopter. She was happy, and my kids were happy. I was overwhelmed, and I was grateful to God for blessing me again with another good job. I was especially blessed because not everyone could get hired at Boeing. Only people with the experience and the knowledge to work for the aeronautical industry can work for Boeing. As we always say in church, God is an on-time guy. He's right on time every time. I had several weeks to go before I was due to report to Boeing to take a physical and to do paperwork.

When I returned to the shipyard, I told my shop foreman I was resigning my position as a shipwright effective the following week. I then broke the news to my coworkers that I had been hired at Boeing Helicopter. I also told the friend whom I had worked with for so many years at the other end of the shipyard. He and my other coworkers were sorry to see me leave. They all expressed surprise that I had been hired at Boeing Helicopter. They knew that not everyone could work at Boeing, only those people with aeronautical experience. I took satisfaction from the fact that these guys were surprised to see that a shipyard worker, someone they worked with for years, had what it took to work at Boeing Helicopter. My coworkers were impressed that I had been hired to work for Boeing. I was very grateful for the opportunity and couldn't wait to get started.

As my last day at the shipyard drew nearer, I thought about my first day, in 1978 when I started in the shipwright apprenticeship program. I thought constantly about my time in the program, my time working on the ships, working in the sawmill, working in the dry dock, docking and undocking ships. I thought about all of the people I worked with at the shipyard, the people who trained me to be a shipwright, my shop foreman, the jobs he'd given me, and my longtime work partner. I thought of all the beautiful days at the shipyard and about the weather. I thought about working down in the dry dock setting in the cradle brocks and the keel blocks for the ships. I thought about getting the dry dock ready for a ship's arrival and about the ship's overhaul. I recalled everything I had accomplished during the years I worked at the shipyard. I even recalled the time I applied for a job as shop foreman and how I believed the job was taken from me. But I got over it because I knew God had a special purpose for me sometime, somewhere. And all I had to do was to be patient and to be faithful to him. And just wait.

As I continued to think about my years at the shipyard, I recalled the accidents. I thought about the many sailors I'd met and about the jobs I'd done on board so many ships. These were stories I could share with my children. I thought about all of that. But the thing I thought about the most was that I was going to miss the guys I worked with. I was going to miss the jobs I'd done in the shipyard. I was going to miss the cold days on a pier sighting in a ship we were docking in the dead of winter. I was also going to miss working on the flight decks of aircraft carriers and helicopter carriers in the summer heat. I never complained about doing my job as a shipwright. I just did it. That was the most important thing to me. I was blessed to have been a part of the Philadelphia Naval Shipyard. But now it was time to move on to another job. I could chalk up my time at the shipyard as another of life's experiences that I could share. I was grateful to God. I had been faithful to him. I trusted God, who showed me that he was always there when I needed him. I knew the shipyard was going to close and I wanted to act early to secure a good job. I didn't want to find myself at the shipyard on its last day and have nowhere to go. I thought ahead. I thought about my family and about my responsibilities, and I knew it was time for me to move on. So I took that step and reached out and applied for another job.

I was starting my new job at Boeing Helicopter, not knowing what I would be doing there or where I would be working. I knew that Boeing was a very good company and that it would be just as good as the Philadelphia Naval Shipyard, if not better. It was now 1986 and my years at the shipyard were over. I was very eager to start at Boeing Helicopter. On my first day, I sat down to fill out all the necessary paperwork. Then I had a meeting with the plant manager, one of the persons who reviewed my application, and he told me he was very pleased to have someone with my experience working at Boeing Helicopter and in his division. He was the plant manager for the helicopter division.

That was where I would be working. My job title would be transmission mechanic B, and my duties would be to catalog the parts for transmissions, to clean the parts, to build transmissions, and to test them. I was very pleased when the plant manager told me he wished everyone who worked in the transmission shop had my experience. I was eager to get to the shop to see how things were done there. After I had finished the paperwork and had taken my physical, the plant manager escorted me to the shop. He introduced me to the foreman and then to all of the workers. I noticed I was blessed again. There was only one African American working in the transmission shop, and I made the second. I felt pretty good about that because the plant manager had told me he wished everyone who worked in that shop had my experience. I realized my experience had gotten me the job.

Once I got settled in the shop, I discovered several guys working there had no aviation experience and had been hired through relatives. I asked some of the men where they had worked before they started at the transmission shop, and several of them said they had been at part stores or had worked as auto mechanics and had been hired at Boeing because relatives pulled strings. They assumed I must have known someone to get hired in the shop. "It wasn't who I knew. It was what I knew that got me hired to work here in the transmission shop," I told them. I found out from my coworkers that the transmission shop was a closed shop and that everyone at Boeing Helicopter wanted to work there, mainly because the place was climate-controlled. The temperature and the air quality had to be just right for the building and the installation of the transmissions. I think that's the reason my coworkers asked me how I was able to get hired to work in the shop when so many other people at Boeing had tried and had failed. I felt very blessed.

When I mentioned my work experience to the guys, most of them were greatly impressed to learn that I had been in the military and that transmission work had been part of my job as a jet mechanic. I had worked on jet engines, helicopters, and helicopter transmissions, so almost nothing in the shop was new to me. The only exception was building the transmissions for Chinook helicopters. By the end of the day I had a list of all the tools I would need to perform my job, and I already had just about every one of them since those were the tools I used when I was in the military. The only thing I needed to buy was a nice toolbox where I could store all of the aviation tools I already owned.

I felt pretty good about my first day in the transmission shop. I got to meet a lot of the guys and to find out about the people I would be working with. I quickly learned the procedures in the shop. All of the parts for the transmissions would be unpacked and cataloged. Then the parts would be cleaned and would be placed on a table. Finally they would be assembled as per a bar chart. As each part was assembled, an inspector would oversee the operation. I found this interesting; I had done some of these things as a jet mechanic in the navy. I got a tour of the whole shop including the test cells, the area where we would test each transmission. I also saw the area where we would disassemble transmissions when they came in for overhauls. The shop was a pretty nice size but had only about thirty-five workers. I understood now how attractive that shop was to a lot of people who worked at Boeing Helicopter. It had relatively few employees and was climate-controlled because of the parts used in the manufacturing of transmissions. That is why many people at Boeing wanted to work there. I was very blessed to have the opportunity to work in the transmission shop. I was all ears, eager to learn something new.

I was very excited when I arrived the next day. I wondered what I would be doing in the transmission shop. This was my first real workday at Boeing, and since I was the new guy in the shop, I had to start at the bottom. My job was to clean and to degrease transmissions parts before installation. The job was quite boring at first, but I finally got accustomed to it. I learned a little more about the procedures in the shop as the weeks went by. I was given several duties, but my main job for the time being was to clean and to degrease parts that would be used to assemble the transmissions. I had to learn several cleaning procedures, and I caught on quickly to everything I was taught. My experience as a jet mechanic in the navy had a lot to do with how quickly I learned the transmission shop's operations.

After about six months at Boeing Helicopter, I asked my shop foreman if I could now work out on the tables building transmissions. I said I was ready to learn how the bar chart and the inspection process worked, and I pointed to my background in the aviation field. I thought I was worth more than just cleaning parts. I knew I had to start somewhere, but I thought I had done that long enough, and I wanted to begin building the transmissions and eventually to learn the operation of the test cells where the transmissions were checked out. My foreman told me he would consider my request and would give me his decision after speaking to his superiors, and I greatly appreciated that. Within a day or two, the foreman told me he would be more than happy to have me work out in the production area along with another transmission mechanic so I could learn the procedures for building the transmissions for Chinook helicopters.

I was grateful for the opportunity. I would be the only African American working in the production area building the Chinook transmissions, and I wanted to make sure I performed skillfully and professionally; I had the same mind-set I had in the military as an aviation jet mechanic. I knew my new job building the transmissions would not be easy, but with my experience I was sure I could overcome any obstacle I would face. I was ready to experience something new. When I began working in the production area, I started out by cataloging all the parts required in building transmissions. Then I worked my way up to assembling the parts once they were cataloged. Each transmission was different, though some of the parts were similar. With my aviation experience, I found the work very easy. I learned the procedures for building the transmissions very quickly—I think a lot more quickly than most of the guys in the shop. Some of them did not have the aviation experience I had, and it may have taken them longer to learn the procedures.

I worked with other transmission mechanics, guys who had been there for a very long time. They showed me the correct procedures, and I was soon able to assemble parts and to build transmissions myself. The inspectors would check every operation I did in building the transmissions, making sure it was done according to the bar chart. After several weeks, my foreman congratulated me on my performance, and I was happy to hear that. I quickly learned the procedures for building the transmissions for the Chinook helicopters, and my foreman was very pleased. I asked him one day if I could learn the procedures for testing the transmissions in the test cells. Another transmission mechanic operated all of the cells. He had done this for quite a few years and was very knowledgeable about the process. Every test cell was different. Each was designed to test only a particular transmission. I asked my foreman if I could work along with this mechanic to learn the operation of all the test cells. I've always wanted to learn as much as I possibly can. I loved my job at Boeing and was grateful to have it. I was also grateful to be the only African American working in the production area of the transmission shop, but I wanted to do more than assemble transmissions. I wanted to be a test cell operator and to check the transmissions, and I knew it was just a matter of time before I got that opportunity. The opportunity was there, and all I had to do was to reach out and grab it.

Finally, that opportunity came. One day I had finished assembling a transmission, had placed it on a cart, and I had wheeled it out to the test cell area. The test cell operator asked me to give him a hand. He had spoken to the shop foreman, and the foreman had given him the okay to train me in the operation of the test cells. I was overwhelmed to be given the opportunity. This was something I had long wanted to do. I continued to build transmissions. After completing one, I would take it to the test cell area. Then, with the help of the test cell operator, I would install the transmission in the test cell. I would work along with him, setting up everything and starting the test on the transmission.

I'll never forget how loud the test cells were. I was reminded of my days as a jet mechanic when we overhauled jet engines before putting them back in the helicopters. We would take the engines out to a special open area on the base to start them and to run tests. The noise was deafening. And this was out in the open. Now I was testing a helicopter transmission in a test cell. The noise was just as loud but in an enclosed area. I was used to this, however, because I had experienced it so many times as a jet mechanic in the navy. I continued building transmissions, testing them in the test cells, removing them from the test cells, and checking the gears and the bearings for defects. Then I would reinstall everything in the transmission and would put the transmission back in the test cell for a final test run, using preservation oil instead of regular oil to run the transmission. With that, the test of the transmission was completed.

So my job consisted of building, testing, taking apart, checking, and retesting the transmissions and ensuring that they were running according to specifications. I always used to say that an aircraft can't stop on a cloud to fix a problem. In other words, the construction, installation, and testing of a jet engine or a helicopter transmission must be perfect. Every part and function of an aircraft must be right before the aircraft leaves the ground. Sure, you'll have mishaps and human error. We make mistakes and forget things. That's just the way it is. But in the aviation field and in the aeronautical industry, we strive to alleviate human error as much as possible. One day in the shop a transmission was damaged as it was being tested in a test cell. The mechanics found out something had been left in the transmission. While the transmission was being reassembled, a screw got loose or was left in, and that caused damage. I thought about how dangerous it would be if something like that happened while an aircraft was flying. I knew things like that had happened in the past. After this incident, I thought about ways to prevent such a mishap from happening again.

Boeing encouraged employees to submit suggestions that the company would review. Boeing would compensate employees based on the cost savings their suggestions produced for the company. One night in 1987 I sat down at my drafting table and drew up a tool that could be used when assembling a certain part of a transmission. This tool would prevent anything from falling into the transmission. I noted the uses of the tool, how it should be used, and its cost-effectiveness and presented my suggestion for review. Several weeks later I was given an award for designing this tool. Once I had received the award, I went home and designed another tool to be used on a different transmission. The design was similar to the one for the first tool. I received another award in 1990 for another tool I designed for the suggestion program. I continued to submit suggestions and received other awards from Boeing.

I was very pleased to get them, but I wasn't thinking at the time. After I'd left Boeing, I realized I should have patented those tool designs and regretted not doing it.

I received quite a few awards from Boeing for my outstanding performance in the transmission shop. I was even considered for shop foreman. My foreman had recommended me for training to become a supervisor in the transmission shop. He did this based on my experience, my work habits, and my performance. He encouraged me to apply for a better position, and I appreciated his suggestion to the heads of the shop that I would be a good candidate for supervisor training. I enrolled in other training courses at Boeing that I thought would benefit me in the helicopter division. I was pleased to take part in these programs and classes and to add to my store of knowledge.

Finally, in 1992, I was named Employee of the Month for my outstanding performance in the helicopter division. I was overwhelmed to receive this award. I think my shop foreman and my shop head looked at my performance and realized how deserving I was of the honor. I believe I was the first African American to have been given the award. I continue to think about that and wonder if any other African American in the Boeing helicopter division received that award after I had left. I thank God for the honor. I thank him for the wisdom and the ability he gave me. At a dinner in Delaware County, Pennsylvania, one of the plant managers presented me and a few other workers with awards for being named Employee of the Month in our divisions. I was greatly honored to take part in that event.

I tell guys today, "The sky's the limit. You can go wherever you want to go. You can work wherever you want to work. It all depends on how much you want it. The training is there. The schooling is there. All you have to do is to reach out for it." God blessed me with my abilities, and I thank him for that. I love to share my story and to train and to help people. I always tell kids, "Yes, you can." We have had an African American president. I'm sure that as a young man he never thought he would be president of the United States. But because of his ability, because of his training, because of his desire, he became president. Because of my desire, because of my want, I have achieved many honors. And this did not end at Boeing. There were a lot more to come.

After receiving the Employee of the Month award in 1992, I continued working in the transmission shop in the helicopter division. I continued building and testing transmissions for the Chinook helicopters. I continued learning about the test cells we used to test transmissions and got very good at this. I became adept at building transmissions, taking them apart, and testing them, and my shop foreman was pleased at my accomplishments. He asked me to train people in the operation of the test cells. The person who had trained me was getting ready to retire, and I was one of the few people who knew how to operate all the test cells. That was why I was asked to train others. I felt honored to have that opportunity. I took my job very seriously.

Around this time the work got slower in the transmission shop. We were not building or overhauling many transmissions. When I started working at Boeing in 1986, the company had already completed most of its contracts to build helicopter transmissions. Now we were getting close to the end of the remaining contracts. My coworkers and I wondered how long we would be working in the transmission shop. However, Boeing and the Bell Helicopter Company had a joint contract for the production of a new aircraft, the V-22 Osprey. Boeing would be doing a pretty good amount of the work for the Osprey.

I was remained concerned about my job status. Would I still have my job in the transmission shop? Where would I go if Boeing laid me off? We still had a little bit of work coming in from time to time. Transmissions would arrive for overhauls, so we kept busy, but I still wondered how much longer I would be working in the transmission shop. I found out I would not get laid off immediately. The worst-case scenario was that I would get bumped into the labor pool. I would have to work as a laborer or as a janitor until the shop called me back or until I was forced onto unemployment. This was a sobering prospect, but I kept a cool head and continued to do my work, building and testing transmissions, and didn't think too much about the future. I knew that God was in control and that he would keep me where I was or that I would go wherever Boeing had me work. I put my trust in God and left it at that.

I finally learned that I was being bumped and that I was to report the following Monday to work in the labor pool as a janitor. I knew the pay would be less, but I would still be working at Boeing. I reported to the labor pool and was given my duties as a janitor. I was to clean eleven or twelve bathrooms at night. Working the night shift as a janitor felt degrading, but this at least was a job and I had a family to support. I had to do whatever I had to do.

I was comfortable with the job for the time being and believed things would eventually pick up and I would get called back to the transmission shop. It was just a matter of time. I hung in there and continued to do my job as a janitor. I kept my head up high, did what I had to do, and looked forward to that day when I got called back to do what I liked to do best, building and testing helicopter transmissions. Finally, after working in the labor pool for a month or so, I got called to work in another area of Boeing, and I took that job. I was blessed to be called there, because I was getting almost the pay I had been getting as a transmission mechanic but a little bit more than a laborer's pay. I was happy to move out of the labor pool and to finally stop working as a janitor, cleaning bathrooms. That wasn't me. Sometimes we have to do what we have to do to provide for our families. I did just that. To my amazement, I was eventually told to report back to the transmission shop. Several transmissions had to be overhauled, and it looked like I would have quite a bit of work for some time. I was very happy to be back home in the transmission shop building and testing transmissions.

The work was steady, I got plenty of overtime, and it seemed I would remain in the transmission shop for a little while longer. My coworkers, my shop foreman, and the shop head were happy to see me back because they knew I loved my job and was very good at it. I worked hard every day, building transmissions, testing them in the test cells, taking them apart after testing them, checking the gears, reinstalling the transmissions in the test cells, doing final preservation runs in the cells, and finally getting the transmissions approved to be sent out and installed in aircraft. As the months passed, I remained in the transmission shop and continued to make myself useful by presenting several more suggestions to the Boeing Company. I saw a lot of new ways to do things, so I put the ideas down on paper and presented them. I received several more awards for my suggestions. I continued to observe operations and used what I discovered to suggest things that could benefit Boeing. I loved my job. I loved what I achieved working at Boeing. I just wanted to continue doing what I was doing for Boeing.

As the months went by, the workload at the transmission shop again decreased, and I wondered if I might be laid off. Finally, I learned that I was being bumped once again, that I was leaving the transmission shop and going to work in another area at Boeing. But this time I wasn't going to work in the labor pool but was going to work across the road on the V-22 Osprey. I was very excited about that. For the first time I would be able to work on an aircraft that Boeing designed and manufactured. I was sad to leave the transmission shop, but I was very happy to be given an opportunity to work on a V-22 Osprey. I felt privileged to have that opportunity, and I thanked God for another blessing.

I think I was assigned to work on the V-22 Osprey because of my experience as a jet mechanic and an aircraft mechanic in the navy. Several other guys who worked at the transmission shop didn't get that opportunity. After getting my new assignment, I packed up my gear and my toolbox and all my equipment and headed across the road to work on the V-22 Osprey. This was an important moment for me. This would be the first time since my navy days that I would be able to work on an aircraft. I didn't know what the work would entail, but I was sure I would be taught the things I had to do. I was ready for it. And I thanked God for another blessing; I could very well have been laid off but not this time. This time I had the chance to work on the V-22 Osprey. This was an honor because not too people were qualified to work on a brand-new aircraft designed and built by Boeing and Bell Helicopter. And I could tell people I had a part in building the V-22 Osprey. I was eager to start working on the V-22.

I had never worked across the road in the plant where all of the helicopters were manufactured and was very excited about working there. This was a very large plant, and a lot of things were happening in that branch of Boeing. I knew I would find this project interesting. It didn't matter to me what part I played in building the V-22 Osprey. I was delighted to be able to work on that aircraft. The production process on that side of the road was completely different from the operation in the transmission shop. In the shop we built and tested the transmission for the Chinook helicopters. In this plant the transmissions were installed in the helicopters, as were the engines after the helicopters were manufactured and overhauled. This was a very big operation and many people worked there. Still, I'm sure they would have loved to work at the transmission shop, mainly because the shop was climate controlled. The air had to be a certain temperature because we couldn't afford to have the gears and the bearings rust. The temperature had to be just right in the winter and the summer.

The plant on the other side of the road was a completely different world. It was cold. I felt like I was working in a gigantic hangar. There were heaters, but the place wasn't as comfy as the transmission shop. That was something I had to get used to. That wasn't much of a problem for me because I had worked in many environments and could adapt to any situation, go wherever I had to go, and do whatever my job entailed. This was what I loved to do. I looked forward to working in a huge hangar, where I might learn something new, to seeing the new aircraft, and to having a part in manufacturing it. It didn't matter to me whether my role was big or small. I was blessed to be given the opportunity of a lifetime and to work on a V-22 Osprey. While I was there, I also worked on the Chinook helicopters, getting them ready for final production and for testing. I felt almost like I was back in the navy as I worked on the Chinook, Sikorsky helicopters, and Cayman helicopters as well as the V-22 Osprey.

My duties varied. One day I might be working on the Chinook; another day I might be working on the V-22 Osprey. Sometimes I would spend a week or two on one and then switch over to the other. My assignment depended on the workload and the manpower, but I had constant work between the two aircraft. I even got the chance to see test flights. It was quite interesting, and there was a lot to learn. I loved working on the V-22 Osprey and the Chinook helicopters. I loved it to the point where I did not want to return to the transmission shop. I was hoping I might stay on that side of the road working on the Chinooks and on the V-22s. Because of my experience as a plane captain, an aircraft mechanic, and a jet mechanic, I had no problem with the work on either aircraft. No matter what job I was given, I completed it in a professional manner.

I looked forward to working on the Chinook and the V-22 Osprey.

Then one day I was laid off. The layoff notice hit me pretty hard. I didn't know what I was going to do or where I would go from there. I had started working at Boeing in 1986, and in 1993 I was done there. I decided to pray about it and to ask God to direct me to another place. I refused to stay down. I got up and I thanked God for saving me once again. God had brought me through that trial and others, and I didn't quit. God had blessed me with plenty of experience in several fields, and I knew he would prevail. He would find something very special for me once again. God had brought me through so much, and I had faith that he would bring me through this storm to peace once again. That's because I knew God is a deliverer. Yes, I did worry a little bit. I worried about providing for my family, but I knew my God would provide for me. I believed that.

Christians go through lots of ups and downs, and sometimes Satan will disrupt life. But God is always there to protect us and to get us out of any difficulty. We must believe and trust in God to deliver us. If we fall, he will pick us up. If we have faith in what God can do, we will prevail. I was gone from Boeing, but that wasn't the end of the world for me. I said to myself, *Satan, you're a liar, because God has got my back.* I continued to think positive thoughts, to pray, and to thank God for all the blessings he had given me. I also thanked him in advance for the things he hadn't done yet but would do for me in the future.

Sometimes we must put things behind us and move forward—step out in faith and cross over the Jordan. Though I had lost my job at Boeing, I knew God would provide for me. I had always trusted in God, and I knew God would meet my every need. And yes, God had given me gifts, the skills I had acquired. Though I had been put through the ringer, I had been blessed with a lot of things. Some people might have said I had failed, but I knew if I trusted in God I wouldn't fail. My mother instilled this in me when I was a young boy, and I thank her for that and I thank God as well.

So, putting Boeing behind me, I looked up to God and asked Him to guide me. I was sure I would find a job I could retire from. That had been my goal at Boeing, but I knew life must go on. I was able to collect unemployment, which was fine. I continued to use my experience in remodeling and found plenty work. I never worried much about making money or about providing for my family, because God had blessed me with talents and experience, and so I always had a way of making money. I thank God for giving me those gifts. Soon after leaving Boeing, I landed quite a few remodeling jobs. I had plenty of work to keep me busy and plenty of money to make, and I thanked God for that.

One year I went out Christmas shopping and bought my son language tapes. He was about eleven years old at the time, but for some reason I thought he might be interested in learning other languages. I thought he might learn other languages like I did, but I never knew he studied those tapes. I love classical music and learned to love opera as a young boy in school. And I thought for some reason my son would get that gift and would learn to appreciate classical music himself. Time passed and my three children were in high school. My son had continued to study the language tapes, though I still didn't know that. I found out sometime later that his studies had paid off for him. That was the gift I gave my son. We always like to leave our kids something we've done, something we've enjoyed, hoping maybe our children will love what we love. We also want them to be the best in whatever they do. I instilled in my children the importance of education and always stressed how far learning could take them.

It was now 1993. I had no problem providing for my family. I collected unemployment and had plenty of remodeling jobs. I was doing pretty well. A friend of my oldest sister knew I had been laid off. I remembered him seeing my sister when we were young. One day he told me he could get me a job as a carpenter at the company where he worked. He said with my experience as a carpenter and a cabinetmaker, I could easily get a job there, especially because the company thought highly of him, so his recommendation would carry a lot of weight. He spoke to the owner of the company and told me they would give me a call in a couple of days. I was happy to hear that. I thought, *Wow, he must have some clout.*

CHAPTER 21

In a few days, I received a call from Sid Levy, the owner of Levy Construction, and his son, Simon Levy. I spoke with father and son for an hour or so about my experience as a carpenter. The two men offered me a job as a carpenter with their construction company and explained what the job would entail. This was a small, privately owned, nonunion company. They asked if I could start work the following Monday and said they would give me a detailed job description then. I felt blessed to land a job as a carpenter with a construction company. This was something I had always wanted to do. When I was in high school in the sixties, I had taken a test to get into the carpenters union in South Philly. At that time, sad to say, there were no African Americans working in the union. The owner of a construction company offered me a job once I got into the union, but I was not able to do that. As a carpenter, I felt blessed to be able to work for Levy Construction, which was nonunion, and I thanked my sister's friend, who put a word in for me. I also thanked God for making it possible for me to be hired.

The following Monday I reported to Levy Construction in Audubon, New Jersey. I was happy to get started and was curious to find out the type of work the company did and what my job would entail. Simon Levy outlined the work I would be expected to do. The work included several phases of carpentry, and with my experience, I had no problem with that. I started out working alone. Simon showed me schools in South Jersey where the company had done renovations and where punch lists had been posted. A punch list is a list of items that must be corrected. Simon wanted me to take care of these items. I got started and went into a couple of places and corrected the issues. Upon completing the work, I would notify Simon. Each day he would give me jobs. I would go in to a school, take care of the punch list items, and move on to another location. I did these punch list jobs for a month or two and completed the work without problems.

The company and the schools were satisfied with my work. I loved what I was doing and took pride in completing the jobs quickly and professionally. I'm sure my boss recognized that. Simon continued to count on me to do punch list jobs. I hadn't had a chance to meet the rest of the company's workers because I was too busy fixing work done in the past. Punch list items had to be corrected, and that was my job from the time being. I knew eventually I would meet and would work with the other carpenters from Levy Construction. Finally, there were no more punch list jobs to do. Levy Construction had started new jobs, and I was able to work with many of the other carpenters employed by the company. I was happy to meet these guys, and they were happy to meet. They had heard good things about me from my sister's friend. He had told them I was an excellent carpenter. I knew my job as a carpenter, and I put all I had into my work and did every job in a professional manner. My work spoke for itself. Sid and Simon Levy saw my professional performance on the punch list jobs. All of the guys who worked for Levy Construction wanted a chance to work with me to see how much I knew.

I noticed the company had only two African Americans workers—the gentleman who had mentioned me to the owners, and another guy. Both were laborers; neither was a carpenter. I came to the company waiting for the opportunity to show what I knew, just as I had at every other place I'd worked. I continue to thank God for giving me the knowledge and the ability to do the jobs I have done and to absorb every bit of information I could get from them. I've studied in schools, I've got many accomplishments under my belt, and I've worked hard to learn and to understand lots of things, and I thank God for that. I've also tried so many times to tell the younger guys, "Get a trade. Learn something, and you'll never go broke," and I say that because of my experience.

I was never out of work for long. I was always busy because of the many skills I acquired. I made it my business to keep working and to make money. The men at Levy Construction were excited about this new guy and wanted to work with me, and they finally got a chance to do it. They got to see my skills, to see what I knew, to see the way I worked, to see my professionalism. I hoped this would matter to them, because I noticed some of the guys didn't have the same drive I had. I hoped to see that change as I worked for Levy Construction. I wanted to show the other African American guys who worked for the company that they could be carpenters, that they could learn as much as they wanted to learn about the carpentry trade and could do as well as I had done as an African American carpenter.

I worked with the other carpenters on jobs at schools, at municipal buildings, and at colleges. Levy Construction did all types of construction including interior and exterior renovations and concrete work. I enjoyed working with the other carpenters employed by the company. I also worked with quite a few subcontractors—the electrician subs, the plumbing subs, the fire control subs, even some of the concrete and flooring subs. We were like a little family; the company was small, and we were all pretty close to one another. We respected each other and worked together to get a job done on time. Sometimes we had disagreements, but we always finished the job. That was the formula for a good company: getting along with other people, working together, and getting the job done on time and in a professional manner. I enjoyed every bit of it. Sid and Simon Levy were compassionate people. They cared about the men who worked for them. Many people wanted to work for Levy Construction because of the compassion the father and the son showed for the men they employed. The owners would always help their workers whatever the situation might be, and the men respected them for that.

I have always looked back at what God has brought me through, and he has brought me through a lot from the time I was a young boy growing up in inner-city Philadelphia to the time I was a grown man going from job to job to provide for my family. I bless God for every bit of that. I mentioned earlier that I had bought my son language tapes when he was eleven years old. When he was in high school, I got a phone call from one of the editors of the *Courier Post* newspaper, who asked to speak with my son. When I asked him why, he said my son had taken the National Latin Exam and had aced it. He said he wanted to ask my son how he did that. At the time, many colleges were contemplating eliminating Latin courses, and the editor was writing an article about the issue. I gave the phone to my son. After speaking to my son, the editor spoke with me again. He had asked my son how he was able to ace the National Latin Exam taken by more than 250,000 high school students, and my son had replied, "All you have to do is listen." I thought that was impressive. I never thought he would take the language tapes I'd given him so seriously. In fact, long before he finished high school he was able to speak and to interpret several languages. I had always told my children, "Once you learn other languages, you will never have to worry about a job." Now I knew my son had listened to me. He also taught himself violin in high school. He had worked his way up and played first violin in the orchestra. The violin is a very hard instrument to learn, but he persisted. I felt very good about that because he had listened.

The Bible says, "Teach the children the way of the Lord." I taught my son and my daughters a lot about the Bible, a lot about God. I taught them a lot about life and told them they could be whoever they wanted to be. A few months after my son aced the National Latin Exam, he was nominated by several people at his school to become a student ambassador representing the United States. I thought it was an honor for him to visit other countries and to live with people there. He accepted that honor. I accepted it as his parent and made it possible for him to take that trip to Europe and to be a student ambassador. With the help of my boss at Levy Construction, my son made that trip. When he did, I realized he was the only African American nominated for the honor. I was proud of all my son's accomplishments, and I thank God for blessing me, my son, and my family. My grandfather played fiddle. He passed his fiddle on to my older sister, who tried to learn to play. Later, she noticed her son had the love and the passion to learn the instrument. Her son played the violin for a time. I have since asked my son to teach me the violin, because I have a passion to play it along with him and my nephew before I leave this life. It's my bucket list item. I trust God to help me do that since he has already brought me through so much.

I thanked God for my job at Levy Construction. I knew that eventually my job description would change and that I would make a big difference for the company. That was my goal. I continued working with the rest of the carpenters at Levy Construction. We did renovations to schools, municipal buildings, and colleges. We also did new buildings, additions to schools and to municipal buildings, and police stations. We kept busy all the time, and I was blessed never to be laid off. A few guys were laid off in the winter when work was slow, but I was always able to work throughout the year. I might have a day or two off, but then Levy Construction would always find work for me to do. Most of the time, it was punch list work, but it was still work. I believe Levy Construction kept me working because of my professionalism. Sid and Simon didn't want to lose me, so I worked from job to job, happy and contented.

One year Levy Construction was awarded a job in Riverside, New Jersey. We were hired to put an addition on the municipal building and to do an interior renovation. Once we completed the roof of the addition, I was asked to work with John, one of the foremen, on the interior renovation until completion. This was the first time we had worked together, just he and I. Before we started our first day together, I told him, "When we complete this job, there will be no punch lists." We shook on it and agreed we would finish this job without a punch list. He and I were the only two who would be working this job, and there was no reason for a punch list since we were both professional carpenters.

My foreman and I worked on the renovation for weeks, and as time went by, we became accustomed to each other's work habits. We worked well together. We appreciated each other's professionalism. I felt very good about this. I recalled working with a good friend for many years at the shipyard. He and I became accustomed to each other's work habits and worked well together. The foreman and I were developing the same relationship as we worked on the Riverside municipal building. We enjoyed each other's company, we enjoyed each other's technique and how we would do things, and we agreed not to disagree, and to get the job done in the most professional manner. We saw eye to eye. That's the way we worked. There was no obstacle we couldn't conquer. If there was a problem, we would get each other's advice about how to approach it. We came to a happy conclusion, and we got the job done each time. I felt very good about working with this foreman. John wanted to see what I knew, to observe my work habits, and I think he was very comfortable working with me. He told me he would work with me anytime.

As we neared completion of the job, we had one big area to do. In some of the offices we were to install arched windows. This was a historic building, and the township wanted everything to be pretty much the same as it had been for years but slightly more modern. John and I started to install the big arched windows. One day people from a newspaper arrived to do a report on the history of Riverside and the municipal building. John and I were working in the building, and photographers were taking pictures as we installed the windows. We were in quite a few of the pictures that were taken, and I thought it was exciting to be doing the renovations to this historic building.

Once we completed the windows, there was work to be done in a bathroom, and the company did not have a contractor available to do the ceramic tile in the room. One day when Sid Levy came to check on the progress of the job, he asked me if I could do the ceramic tile. It was a nice-size bathroom, and I told him I could do the tile on the walls and on the floor. He asked me to make a list of materials I would need and to give it to him so he could get those things for me. The company did not have anyone who could install ceramic tile, so this was an opportunity for me to show what else I could do. I felt very good about that, and I thanked God for all the knowledge and experience I had. I had always been able to obtain and to keep jobs because of my knowledge and experience in many fields. The tile installation was flawless. Officials were pleased with how the bathroom turned out. The renovation was almost completed. All we had left was some exterior work. Then the job would be ready for the punch list inspection.

John and I returned to finish a few items before the final inspection. The women who worked at the municipal building had made a cake for us. It was topped with a picture of a teddy bear with a tool belt and a hammer. Next to the teddy bear the ladies had added a notation saying, "Job well done—no punch lists." My foreman and I appreciated that. Once we were finished, the punch list inspection took place. When the architect and a township official had finished the inspection, there was no punch list. I looked at the foreman and he looked at me, and we shook hands. "Yes, it can be done," I said. The job was completed, the township was completely satisfied, and I was told the mayor wrote a letter to Levy Construction thanking the company for the renovation to the municipal building that John and I had done. I thought this was an honor. Levy Construction was very pleased to have gotten a letter like that. I was very pleased. The company realized two guys had finished the renovation of a building without a punch list. This stuck with me for years after we completed the job. From that time until the day I retired, I would tell the foreman, "Yes, jobs can be done without a punch list or with a minimal punch list. Yes, it can be done. If two of us can do it, I know the company could do it on every job."

I moved on to other jobs with the foreman. John said he was happy to work with me. Sometime later, Sid Levy called me into his office, told me the company's construction superintendent was leaving, and asked if I would be interested in taking the position. I was shocked at the offer. I had been with the company perhaps a year and was the company's only African American carpenter. Sid and Simon explained what the job would entail and asked me to give it some thought. They told me to let them know my decision by the following week. When I went home that evening, I was very excited. I explained the offer to my wife. I had to think hard about whether to take the position. I was the only African American carpenter at the company. I didn't know how things would work out for me in that position, mainly because I came from the outside. I hadn't been with the company long. Other men had been with the company for years, and to my knowledge, none of them had been considered for the position. I prayed about it and made my decision, and I was ready to give the owners of Levy Construction my decision on Monday when I returned to work. I looked at all the things God had brought me through. I thanked him for everything he had given me, and I continue to do that.

On Monday I went in to see Sid and Simon and told them I would be delighted and honored to take the position as construction superintendent. They were happy and told me they would work with me as much as possible until I was able to perform the job as I should as a construction superintendent. I was thankful to hear that. Once I took the position, I worked with the current superintendent, who detailed what would be required of me. I rode with him for a few weeks, and he showed me the ropes. I was happy that I had a new job, an important one for a small company. I knew a lot of people in the company would probably dislike the fact that I had been chosen as their superintendent, but I felt could handle any challenge. I remembered Philippians 4:13: "I can do all things through Christ which strengthens me." That's one of my favorite scripture verses, and I keep it in my heart.

The company's workers were surprised that I was going to be their superintendent. Many of the men were dissatisfied. Some people are never satisfied. This looked like the perfect opportunity for me to make a difference. I would represent Levy Construction wherever I went and be a model for the other African American men who worked at the company. They would see that I got this position because of my ability, my professionalism as a carpenter, the way I dealt with people, and how I expressed myself. They would look at that and understand they could do the same thing.

I thank God for the opportunity that I got to be the construction superintendent for Levy Construction. I knew I would go a long way in time. I resolved that every day I would do my job as superintendent to the best of my ability to show that the company could do good work. That was my goal. I wanted to make a difference for the men and for the owner and to show them what I stood for. I think the Levis already understood me enough to have offered me the job as construction superintendent. I believe they saw something in me that would make a difference for Levy Construction. I was very grateful for that. I had been trained for several weeks by my predecessor. He had retired, and now the job was mine. I thought my job as construction superintendent was a gift from God. I thought this was something special, and I vowed to do my best as the first African American construction superintendent for Levy Construction. I also realized that quite a few of the workers were not pleased that I was their superintendent. I tried not to let that bother me, because I knew the owners, not these guys, had offered me the position. This was the decision of the company and not of the men who worked for the company.

I knew I would face so many challenges, and I prepared myself for that. I prayed that God would watch over me and protect me as I did my job as construction superintendent. I did my job like all the other jobs I'd had. I did it in a professional manner. I learned a lot from my foreman. We worked together to get jobs done on time and professionally. Yes, there were struggles at times, but I loved my job as superintendent. I attended my first prebid conference as construction superintendent, and many people were surprised to an African American representing the company. I'm sure many attendees were looking for the former superintendent, and when I showed up at the meeting representing Levy Construction, I could see the confused looks on people's faces. As I attended job meetings, prebid conferences, and construction meetings, I got funny looks from people, but I kept my head up and continued doing my job.

One day I attended a prebid construction meeting at a prison. All visitors entering the building were asked to surrender their licenses and were issued temporary badges from the corrections facility. After the meeting we returned the badges to an officer, and the officer returned the licenses. Everyone had been cleared to leave, but I was still waiting. The corrections officers told me they could not find my license. I thought that was very odd because when they collected the licenses, I saw them put all the IDs in the same box. I waited twenty to thirty minutes after everyone was gone before the CO finally told me, "Oh, we found your license." When he gave it to me, I looked at him and said, "Thank you. Have a nice day." I understood what this was all about, but I did not let that deter me from my job as an African American construction superintendent. I was blessed to have that position.

Every time I have visited corrections facilities and have seen young men locked up, I have thought how their lives could have been different if they had made better choices. We have all been given minds to decide what is right and what is wrong. If we have been properly raises, we are likelier to make better choices when we grow up. I thank God for the way I was raised. I have always tried to encourage the young, including the young men employed by the companies where I have worked. Levy Construction was a great company to work for. I worked with my boss, who taught me many things about the business. He trusted me and I rewarded that trust with the way I presented myself. I vowed never to let him down, because he gave me the opportunity to make a difference. About a year after I had taken the job as superintendent, Sid Levy passed away and Simon took over the company. Simon and I worked well together, and his instruction made me a better superintendent.

There were still differences between me and a few of the men, but as time passed, our relationship got better. Simon Levy appreciated everything I'd done for the company, and he expressed his appreciation many times. I thank God for that. Simon asked me on several occasions to draw up sketches for him to present to a customer or to an architect. I think he was familiar with my experience as a draftsman. I may have told him about my schooling, so he had no problem asking me to draw up sketches for jobs. He was always pleased with my sketches.

One day a subcontractor who made cabinets and countertops for us asked me if I knew an architect. When I asked him why, he said he was ready to build an addition to his house but needed an architect to draw blueprints to present to his town. When I said I could do it for him, he was excited and surprised. He agreed to my price. The sketches took me about a day to do. He was pleased with the drawings and presented them to his town. His permit application was approved within a few days. He was very excited, and when he shared the news with me, I was happy for him. I was also happy to know that the sketches I drew up for him were acceptable to his town. I saved him a lot of money by drawing up those plans for him, and he was very appreciative. I thanked God that I was able to help someone with the experience and the knowledge God had given me. God has brought me through a lot, and I praise his name and thank him every day for that. Some years went by and I ran into the subcontractor. "You haven't been over to my house to see the addition you drew up for me," he said. When I stopped by, I saw that the addition was built exactly the way I drew it up, and I was very proud of myself for doing that.

Doing the drawings for that addition was inspiring to me because drafting was one of my passions along with interior home remodeling. I didn't have the time to do remodeling once I started working as a construction superintendent, but I still had the desire to do it again. For the time being I was comfortable with my job at Levy Construction, and I was content to know that this would be the job I retired from. I had the opportunity to draw plans for an addition my neighbor wanted on his house. I presented them to my neighbor, he applied for and was granted the permits, and I built the addition from the footings to the final exterior and interior finishes. My neighbors were on vacation while I worked on the addition. When they returned they were pleased with the outcome. On many occasions I have been called a renaissance man. I praise God for blessing me with knowledge and understanding.

As the years passed, I got better at my job as construction superintendent. My boss and I got along very well, and I had a good relationship with all of the men. We continued to get a lot of jobs in the winter and the summer, and the business was flourishing. I had been suffering a lot of pain in my thighs, my legs, and my hips, and I went to see a doctor for a checkup. I realized I needed a hip replacement, but when the doctor reviewed the x-rays he determined I wasn't quite ready. He told me I would know when that time came. I prayed about it and continued with my job, going from job site to job site, attending prebid meetings, construction meetings, and preconstruction meetings. I enjoyed my job very much. God had given me the ability to do the many jobs I had done, and I appreciated that gift. As an African American, I felt blessed to have been offered a job as superintendent of a construction company. I had held that position for several years, and the jobs had gotten bigger and better, and my pay had increased. I felt blessed every day.

One day a friend of my younger daughter had told me I had a voice that was perfect for radio or TV, and he said I should consider doing voice-overs. "What is a voice-over?" I asked him. I did some research and found out a voice-over artist is someone who provides the voice for radio, TV, narrations, messaging, audio books, and much more. I looked online for companies that trained people to become voice-over artists, and I found a company named suchavoice.com. I did an audition by phone, and the company got back in touch with me and set me up for a master class. I began training as a voice-over actor, and when I completed my training, I recorded a demo that I could use to apply for voice-over work. I purchased the equipment I needed to do voice-over work, and I started right away.

I was never one to sit still or to be comfortable with just one thing. I was always open to new and different things, and that was what sparked my desire to be a voice-over artist. I continued working for

Levy Construction and I continued doing my voice-over work. I did the voice-over work in the evenings and on weekends. I've done quite a few auditions for voice 1 2 3 and for voices.com. I've kept at voice-over work since starting it in 2008. Whenever I've had the time I've done auditions for clients through voices.com and voice 1 2 3. I've been very pleased to hear the response I've gotten from clients. I've continued to do voice-over work in my spare time and on weekends because it's my passion. I love to talk on the Mic, and I know one day someone will hire me to do a commercial, a narration, an audio book, or a messaging system. It's just a matter of time, and I stay focused and pray about it constantly. I trust God will someday make a way for me to use the gift of my voice.

After starting voice-over work, I opened a website where people can listen to my demos and give me their reaction or ask about my services. My website is tdvoicetalent.com, and I look forward to people contacting me to do voice-overs for them. I can handle any assignment, and that's why I ask people to send me a script. I'll take it from there.

Once I had begun, I continued with my voice-over work and continued to get feedback. This pursuit looked very hopeful for me. I loved what I was doing and I vowed never to stop. I was taught during my voice-over training that it can a long time to get recognized or to land that first voice-over job. The important thing is never to give up. I continued to think and to act that way. I continued to do auditions after work, during work hours, and on the weekends. I worked as a construction superintendent until the problem with my hip got worse as I climbed in and out of the F 250 truck I drove. I went in to see the orthopedic surgeon. He took x-rays again and said it was time for hip replacement surgery. I went to classes about what to expect after hip replacement surgery. The classes were very helpful because I knew little about the aftermath of this invasive procedure.

I explained to my boss that my recovery would take anywhere from several weeks to two months. Simon Levy was compassionate and caring about my situation, and I was very grateful to have a boss who was so concerned about my condition. He told me that when I recovered, my job would still be available for me and that he hoped and prayed for my speedy recovery so I could return to work. I was thankful for that. Just before the surgery, I prayed to God, asking him to guide the hands of the surgeon and to allow me to recover without any setbacks.

This was the first surgery I had ever had, and I was concerned about how I would react after the operation. The classes I attended before the surgery gave me hope that I could deal with problems after the surgery. I was prepared. When I came to after the surgery, I felt nothing in my legs. They were numb and I was concerned. I thought something had gone wrong. I prayed to God and fell asleep. When I woke up, the surgeon and the physical therapist were standing by my bed. They asked me how I felt and if I could stand up. I felt good and said, "Yes, I can stand up." So I stood up. Then the surgeon and the therapist asked me if I could take a few steps. I asked, "How far?" They opened the door to my room and I walked down the hall for sixty to eighty feet. Then I turned around and came back. The surgeon and the physical therapist were surprised, and they told me that the next morning I could go down to the physical therapy room and go through tests. If I did well on all the tests, I could go home.

As I lay back in my hospital bed, I took a few minutes to thank God for delivering me. I remembered Philippians 4:13, which says, "I can do all things through Christ which strengthens me." Yes, God had given me the strength to get up and to walk. I was able to do that through him. I was doubtful before the surgery, not knowing how things would turn out, but I always kept that scripture verse close to me, trusting in what God could do. God is a healer, a deliverer, and much more. He had brought me through so much, and I was still here. I was released from the hospital the day after my surgery, and I returned home to begin my rehabilitation with the brand-new hip joint. I was in a lot of pain at first. I had a physical therapy nurse visit me two or three times a week. It took pain medicine and I prayed about my situation. In only a few weeks, I was walking with a cane. I had a little limp, but I was grateful that I could get up and walk and that I didn't suffer a lot of pain. Maybe I was the type of person who could endure more pain than others, but I thank God for my delivery. I thank him for healing me; the healing process was very short.

My boss would call me up periodically to check on me. I returned to my church, and people were surprised to see me back so soon after my surgery. Several weeks after I had my hip replacement, I was getting around fairly well, and I wanted to try something I hadn't done in a while. My son had left a pair of inline skates in his room. One day I got those skates, I put them on, went outside, and skated down to the other end of my street. And I came back. I did this several times. My neighbor looked out the window and was surprised to see me skating not long after I had my hip replaced. I fell a couple of times, but I got up and made a few more trips up the street and back just to see if I still had it. And I did. I thanked God for healing me in such a short time. God has brought me through so much, and I continue to thank him for all he has done for me.

As the weeks passed, I got stronger and stronger with my hip replacement. I was able to return to work. My boss was very happy to have me back, and I resumed working as construction superintendent. I picked up where I had left off. It didn't seem like I had been away that long. All the men were happy to see me back. I went to church every week, and I was grateful to be healed and to have a good job. I did renovations at my church, and my pastor was pleased with the work I had done. As time went by, my workload grew at Levy Construction, but I didn't mind. After some disagreements, I left my church. Before I left, I prayed about it, and I decided it was time to head somewhere else. I was hurt by some of the things that happened in the church. I felt let down by God's people. I felt a bit of emptiness once I left that church. I felt a lack of something within my spirit. I was out of church for almost a year. I missed the fellowship that I once had in church, and I still had no church home. I would continue to watch church channels, but that wasn't the same as being in church and in fellowship with other Christians.

One day after I crossed a bridge into New Jersey, I was about to drive out to a job site in Glassboro to see how everything was going, but something inside of me said, *Don't go to Glassboro. Go directly to the office.* I thought, *What is this? What's happening?* Once again, I felt a presence say, *Don't go to Glassboro. Go to the office. Now.* At that moment I approached the exit for the office, so I took it. Once I got to the office, I checked my desks for messages, came out, and got into the truck. I wanted to reach Glassboro before the guys finished work for the day so

I could check the status of that job. I started the truck, put it in gear, and nothing happened. The truck wouldn't move. I shut off the truck, started it again, and put it in gear. Nothing. I got out of the truck, looked under it, and was frightened by what I saw. The suspension rod was lying on the ground. I was shocked. I dropped to my knees and I said, "Thank you, Lord, for saving me."

I stopped and I thought about being obedient. And I knew God had tested my obedience. *If I hadn't listened to that voice within me and had headed to Glassboro, I probably wouldn't be here now,* I thought. Had I lost the suspension rod then, I might have been dead, but I was obedient and went to the office. I could only praise God again. "Thank you, God," I said. "Thank you for saving me." I had to share this with my boss. I called the mechanic who usually did the work on the truck, and he said, "This is something that is very unlikely to happen." He could not believe it. That rod was threaded, and it had to unthread itself, which might be easy to do except that there is a bolt that holds it in place. There should have been no way it could come apart. But there was. It did. I believe the grace of God and my obedience saved me. After this experience, I thought God was trying to tell me something.

A friend of my wife had invited us to attend her church. I enjoyed the fellowship and the services, and I continued to go for weeks. Eventually, my wife and I joined that church. It felt good to be back in a fellowship, to be back in the house of God. I met new friends and felt blessed once again. As the months went by, I continued to worship at my newfound church. I participated in Sunday school, Bible study, and church functions. I fellowshipped with other churches and became involved in revivals through these associations. I felt very comfortable at my new church and with the pastor and all of the heads of the church. The fellowshipping was different at my previous church. I realized that every church is different and that everything starts from the top, from the leadership of the church. I was happy to be in the church I was attending. I used my God-given skills as a carpenter to take care of some issues that had to be addressed at the church. They had not been addressed for quite some time. I felt blessed to be able to help out my church with the talent God gave me. I reached out to friends in the construction field to lend a hand with work at my new church, and these guys made themselves available. The pastor and the church members were pleased with the work I'd done. I thank God for blessing me with the ability to do the things I could do. I would always do what I could for my church.

There will always be someone who is never pleased with what you do. People can make life hard for you. They will try to break you and will disrespect you in many ways. That happens all the time because people will be people. The pastor was grateful for the things I'd done in my church, but there were people who were not so grateful and who made life very difficult for me. So as time passed, I considered moving on again. I had been hurt and bruised once again by God's people. *Is it me?* I wondered. *What have I done wrong? I've done the things God has given me the gift to do.* There is no perfect church. Many people go to church and fellowship, but then things happen and they leave. I was in that category, and I prayed to God about it, asking him to put me in the place where he wanted me to be, a place where people show love for one another. Everything begins at the top, to the leader of the church, the pastor. Finally, after thinking about this situation, I decided to resign my membership at that church. My wife and I both left. And again, I found myself lost without a church home.

I missed church; I missed the fellowship with other Christians. But I knew for the time being that I was simply continue to stay in the Word of God. In the evenings and on Sundays, I would watch the church channels. I focused on the messages of the pastors and of the church channels. I knew it was just a matter of time before I found a new church home. At the time I was focusing on my early retirement, something I had to do because I was unable to perform some of my duties due to my two torn rotator cuffs. I was months away from my sixty-second birthday, and I was looking forward to my retirement. After a vacation I returned to the office, and Simon Levy and I discussed upcoming work. He wanted to bring me up to speed on the things I had missed while I had been away on vacation. We would always discuss these things once either of us returned from vacation. When he was done, I told my boss I would be retiring in a few months. I realized this was quite a shock to him. I told me I was too young to retire. All I could say was, "Through the grace of God, I've aged well." I think all of my family members have aged well. I did not look my age, and my physical ability had held up fairly well, so my boss never realized I was as old as I was. In fact, none of the men who worked for the company ever knew I was as old as I was. I thank God for that. I explained my plans to my boss, and he decided to do something special for me. I thanked him for it. But I knew the time had come. I had been working since a very young age. I had held many job titles and had experienced many things throughout my life. I had received many commendations awards. I told my boss I would be available for him anytime if need be. I would transition my way out of the company and would retire in a short time. The days were rough. The guys were sad that I was retiring. Most the contractors, subcontractors, and vendors the company worked with knew me and were all sad to hear that I was retiring from Levy Construction. I was grateful to hear the good things that were said about me by these different people. I never knew so many people cared so much about how I treated them and how I carried out business for Levy Construction. I thank God for that, but I knew it was my time to retire.

I finished my last week for Levy Construction and I was done. I could continue to do the voice-over work I was doing while I was working, but now I had extra time to do whatever I wanted to do every day. I didn't have to get up early to go to work. I could sit in front of my mike and do auditions every day. I was looking forward to that. For months after my retirement, I was still getting up very early, as though I were still going to work. This was because of habit. I had become used to doing this over many years. Now that I was retired, I didn't have to get up early anymore, but I did it anyway because I continued to work on my voice-overs. The auditions were coming in quite frequently, and I would audition every day, every night, as much as possible. I started my voice-over company, TD Voice Talent, and my website, www.tdvoicetalent. com. I've gotten quite a lot of interesting feedback from clients for whom I've done auditions. I kept hoping and praying that one day I would get that first hit for a TV commercial, a radio commercial, or something for a church. I stayed at it every day, but I still missed church. Perhaps that was because some of the auditions I was doing were for churches, but yes, I still missed church.

One day I had spoken to my older sister, and she knew I wasn't in church anymore, so she invited me to her church. Whenever my sister and I talked, she spoke very highly of her church, the Lighthouse of Deliverance Gospel Church in Lindenwold, New Jersey. She also spoke highly of her pastor, Bishop Anthony Harley, and said he instilled so much in the congregation. My sister said I would love being a part of the Lighthouse of Deliverance and would enjoy fellowshipping with her church. She asked me to come to see how I felt. I accepted the invitation, and when I attended the Lighthouse of Deliverance, I noticed the church greeters were very friendly to all who came. The worship was very intense. Bishop Anthony Harley was solid and engaging in his teaching and preaching of God's Word. I felt very comfortable there. I enjoyed all of the services I attended; I enjoyed the fellowship at the Lighthouse of Deliverance Gospel Church. I met quite a few new friends, and everyone was very friendly and easy to get along with. I began to feel very comfortable there. I started to attend the church every Sunday. I made it to Sunday school before church, and I felt very comfortable back in church again.

I looked back at other churches I had belonged to, and I knew there was no perfect church. Sometimes people go from church to church, trying to find the right one for them, but church is within us. And we learn more and more when we go to church, we study the Bible, and we sit under a pastor who's very serious and engaging in teaching and preaching God's Word. We learn more each time we listen to the sermons or we attend Sunday school or Bible study. This was something I enjoyed at the Lighthouse of Deliverance Gospel Church. I looked forward to attending every week. I looked forward to hearing the Word of God, and I looked forward to hearing the teaching and preaching of God's Word by Bishop Anthony Harley. I knew that one day this could very well be my church home. But I thought about it and left it up to God to make that decision for me, to place me where he wanted me to be. As the months passed, I continued to fellowship with Lighthouse of Deliverance Gospel Church every time I could make it there. I enjoyed the company, and I enjoyed the teaching and preaching of Anthony Harley, so I continued to go faithfully to Sunday school and to church. I decided at one point to take a break for a little while. I stopped going for several weeks. Then I was visited by an old friend with whom I used to work, and he mentioned that his wife was a pastor and that she would be preaching at the Lighthouse of Deliverance Gospel Church. And for some reason I thought that was a message for me to return to that church. When I did, I met my old friend and his wife, the pastor. She preached a sermon at the Lighthouse of Deliverance Gospel Church where they were visiting. I enjoyed the message that evening and was eager to return to the church once again. I know the pastor was very happy to see me return.

One Sunday morning I left my house heading to the Lighthouse, and I find myself taking another route. I didn't realize what I was doing at the time, but I ended up at another church—the church where my friend's wife was a pastor. This was St. James Christian Church on Church Street in Sicklerville, New Jersey. I found it very odd that I wound up there because I usually took the same route to Lighthouse of Deliverance Gospel Church every Sunday. For some reason, I ended up at St. James Christian Church. I thought about it, and I said to myself that perhaps this was something God wanted to happen. Perhaps he was leading me to this church. I went in, and the pastor was very surprised to see me. My friend, the pastor's husband, was happy to see me. The whole church welcomed me. It was just like being at the Lighthouse of Deliverance Gospel Church. The welcome was warm and friendly. St. James Christian Church was a small church, not as large as the Lighthouse of Deliverance, but it was a very loving church, and the members showed their love for one another. They also showed their love for all the visitors looking for a church home or coming to fellowship and to hear the teaching and preaching of God's Word.

I was happy to have found a church so close to home, much closer than the Lighthouse of Deliverance Gospel Church. I felt blessed because this was such a wonderful church, and the pastor and the congregation were loving, kind people. I believe everything instilled in the members comes from the top, the leaders of the church. This was something I also noticed at Lighthouse of Deliverance Gospel Church. The teaching and the preaching were very similar. Love and respect for one another were instilled in the members of the church. They knew that Christ loved the church and that God wanted all of us to love one another as Christ loved the church. I continued attending Sunday school, church services, and Bible study at St. James Christian Church under the leadership of Doctor Pastor Linda Bizzelle King. I met new friends—very good people—the officials of St. James, the ministers, the deacons, the evangelists, the profiteers. The people at St. James loved the church, they loved the pastor, and they loved one another. I believe God will, in his time, bless his house when he sees everyone is of one accord under direction of the man or the woman he has anointed to lead the flock. That's why I believe it's very important that pastors preach and teach the fact that God wants unity in every church. He wants all the members and all the leaders of the churches to be of one accord. He understands that people have their differences, but he wants us to love one another as Christ loved the church.

I continued at St. James Christian Church for a few months, and I left it up to God to lead me to where he wanted me to be. One Sunday morning at St. James Christian Church, I decided to become a member. I felt that the time was near and that God had directed me to St. James Christian Church for a purpose. One morning something had prompted me to go in a different direction, and I ended up at St. James Christian Church. I felt blessed and honored to be a member of St. James Christian Church. I had been in several churches under several pastors. I was out of church for a while, not sure where I wanted to be or where God wanted me to be. I sat still for a while. I prayed to God, and I listened for his direction, and this is where God had sent me— St. James Christian Church. Once I became a member of St. James Christian Church, I participated in the men's fellowship and in the men's choir. This was the first time I had ever had the opportunity to be a part of men's fellowship. I enjoyed it. I enjoyed us all coming together and singing and praising God's name in psalms. This is something I believe was instilled in each man at St. James, something instilled by the pastor. In a lot of churches, pastors will tell the congregation, "Don't just come to church; be a part of your church. Be a part of some ministry within your church." I enjoyed the men's choir ministry, and I intended to go further—whatever ministry God led me to at St. James Christian Church.

God has brought me through many trials and tribulations. God has given me knowledge, understanding, and hope. He has a purpose for each of us, and sometimes we need to sit down and ask him, "What is my purpose in life? What is the purpose that you have for me?" And God will let us know. Romans 10:17 says, "Faith comes by hearing and hearing by the word of God." That's important to remember.

Once we have faith and hear the Word of God, we have the strength to go on and to accomplish anything we set out to do. That's why I would like to stress the point that God has brought me through so much. I continue to fellowship with all the members of St. James Christian Church. From time to time, my wife and I visit other churches and fellowship with them, and this is something God wants to see from all of us. He wants us to reach out to one another; to support one another; and to support our pastors, our bishops, our church leaders. He wants us to come together, to praise his name, and to be obedient to him and his covenant. One scripture verse I keep in my heart is Psalm 119:11, which says, "Thy word have I hid in mine heart, that I might not sin against thee." If we all continue to keep God's covenant and his commandments, he will look down on us, and he will bless us and keep us.

It's hard to deal with the temptations we face every day, but we must remember that God also was tempted. His son, Jesus, was tempted, so we are not any different. After going from church to church, leaving this church, joining another church, leaving that church, I've come to realize we must not lean on our own understanding. We must trust God and ask him for whatever we need. After all, God says, "Ask and you shall receive."

I remember those things and so much more that I have been taught, and I love to share the message. God is good. God is an awesome God. He's a deliverer. He's a faithful God, and he's a jealous God. He wants us to have no other god before him. Sometimes we all look at our material possessions and inadvertently put those things in front of us or put them on a pedestal, but that's not what God wants us to do. Those things that we put on pedestals become replacements for God, and that's something God doesn't want us to do. I am very grateful to God for placing me in St. James Christian Church under the leadership of Dr. Linda Bizzelle-King.

I thank God for that. I thank God for her and for the other leaders of the church. I pray to God every day that we will continue to come together as one and to respect and to love our pastor, the woman of God anointed by him to lead us and to teach us God's way. I remain in St. James as a member and continue to fellowship with other churches.

We have stayed together as a church and have continued to support our pastor. When our pastor is preaching at other churches, the men's choir goes with her in support and sings. After I had made her aware that I do voice-overs, my pastor asked me to do a voice-over of the church's history. I was very excited about doing this. My pastor gave me the script to read. I worked on it, and within a day, I recorded the church's history. I used a music bed. Once the work was completed, I gave it to the pastor. She was very happy to have gotten this voice-over so she could present it to the other church members and they could have copies of their church's history.

As always, I continue to bless God and to thank him for giving me the ability to do the things I have done. Not a day goes by without me thanking and praising God for the wonderful gifts he has blessed me with. I thank God for placing me in St. James Christian Church, the Way Station. I also thank God for making me a part of the fellowship at the Lighthouse of Deliverance Gospel Church, where I have so many times heard the teaching and preaching of God's Word by Bishop Anthony Harley. Those looking for a house of worship in the New Jersey area should visit St. James Christian Church, my church home. The pastor is Linda Bizzelle-King. They could also visit the Lighthouse of Deliverance Gospel Church. The pastor is Bishop Anthony Harley, and the church is located in Lindenwold, New Jersey.

Both churches are a part of the House of Judah. Come visit both churches and hear what God has to say to you and find out what God can bring you through. Since being a member of St. James Christian Church, I have been pleased to see that others are reaching out to our young people. Men Empowering Nations, led by evangelist Virgil L. Carman Jr., is a group of people mentoring the young and teaching them the Word of God and good values. Contact this organization at www. menempoweringnations.org. I believe if I can accomplish what I have throughout my life, there is nothing stopping other young people from reaching their goals. I have Men Empowering Nations as a mentor. I believe I can be an inspiration to the young people in that organization.

God wants us to give back to others what he has given us. It may be hard at times, but if we focus on the goal, we can reach it. All we have to do is trust and have faith in God to carry us through the storm as he did for me. We all have a destiny, but sometimes we don't know what it is. We should ask God to tell us what it is, and I believe he will. God says ask and we shall receive. I also believe we should all leave a legacy when we depart this life and while here live on purpose.

As an African American growing up in the inner city, I never once thought I would have accomplished what I have in my lifetime. But God has brought me through so much by his grace and through my faith in him. He has blessed me throughout my life with knowledge and understanding. We sometimes fall, but God picks us up and uses us. Once we confess our sins, God is faithful and just to forgive us. I believe God is always there waiting to hear from us. Nothing is impossible for God. If my faith in God brought me through, God can do the same for all who believe and trust in him. God has a purpose for all of us. Just ask God what his purpose is for you. I will continue to live blessing God for all he has given me.

ABOUT THE AUTHOR

Born and raised in South Philadelphia, Thomas Dykes was one of eight siblings, including a twin sister. He graduated from high school in 1969 and entered the navy the following year, serving as a sailor and attending several naval schools. He became a jet mechanic and a helicopter plane captain and crew chief. After exiting the navy, Dykes gained recognition for outstanding work in several jobs; while working at Boeing Helicopters, he was nominated as Employee of the Month. Dykes went on to work as a construction superintendent until retiring from the Levy Construction Company in Audubon, New Jersey. He and his wife, Linda, have two daughters and one son. Dykes lives in New Jersey and does voice-over work.

Printed in the United States
By Bookmasters